South American Pipe Snake (Aniliidae) (p.29) is the only member of its family and is found in northern South America.

Shield-tailed Snakes and Asian Pipe Snakes (Uropeltidae) (p.30) are found in India and Sri Lanka. They are secretive, burrowing snakes whose natural history is not well known.

Wood Snakes or West Indian Dwarf Boas (Tropidophiidae) (pp.32–34) are found in the West Indies, with a few species in Central and South America.

Round Island Boas (Bolyeriidae) (p.35) are found only on Round Island in the Indian Ocean. There is one surviving species and one other that is probably extinct.

Boas and Pythons (Boidae) (pp.36–72) are sometimes regarded as two separate families. They are found in most of the warmer parts of the world and include many small to medium-sized snakes as well as the well-known 'giant' species.

Typical harmless and back-fanged snakes (Colubridae) (pp.73–178) include three-fifths of all snakes. They are found throughout the world except for the coldest regions and a few small islands. There is great variation in their shapes and sizes and some species are venomous.

Burrowing Asps (Atractaspidae) (pp.179–181) are poorly known burrowing snakes, some of whom are venomous. They are found in Africa and the Middle East.

Cobras, Mambas, Kraits, Coral Snakes and Sea Snakes (Elapidae) (pp.182–210) are all venomous snakes. They are found throughout most of the warmer parts of the world except Europe and Madagascar.

Vipers and Pit Vipers (Viperidae) (pp.211–252) are venomous snakes with long, hinged fangs. They are found in most parts of the world except Australasia and Madagascar.

INTRODUCTION

There are about 2,500 species of snakes and they are found in most of the warmer parts of the world. This book illustrates and describes over 220 of these species. The species have been selected to show the diversity of size, shape and colour among snakes. Included are species from Europe, North America, southern Africa, South-east Asia and Australia – places where the interest in snakes is perhaps greatest.

Only a small proportion of snakes (about 400) are **venomous** and, of those that are, only a handful, less than 100 worldwide, are dangerous to humans. Only Australia has more venomous snakes than harmless ones but, even there, fatal bites are rare. Even venomous snakes rarely attack unless they feel under threat and many cases of snake-bite can be attributed to foolish behaviour on the part of the victim rather than aggression on the part of the snake.

Because of their elongated shape, snakes have had to make several changes to the way they live. These involve unique methods of catching and swallowing their prey (see **Feeding** pp.12–13). They also use their senses differently from most other animals: they are especially sensitive to vibrations and smell and some species can even detect small changes in temperature through unique organs in their faces (see **Senses** pp.10–11).

Many snakes are beautiful. Their scales, often highly polished, are colourful mosaics that sometimes help the snake to blend into its surroundings and sometimes send out warning signals to other animals (see **Defence** pp.14–15).

What are snakes?

Snakes are reptiles, and are closely related to lizards, tortoises, turtles and crocodiles. The reptiles are an ancient class of animals, dating back at least 310 million years with their heyday during the Mesozoic era, 240 to 65 million years ago. Snakes evolved from lizards and were the latest group of reptiles to appear, about 135 million years ago.

All reptiles are 'cold-blooded', a rather inaccurate description that relates to their means of maintaining a body temperature at which they can function properly. In fact, although they cannot produce their own body heat as mammals can, they prefer to operate at about 25–30°C, depending on species, and can maintain their bodies at a remarkably stable temperature by shuttling between warm and cool places. In cold weather, or in the early morning, they will often bask in the open to absorb as much of the sun's energy as possible, whereas in very hot conditions they seek shelter beneath stones or in burrows and are most active at night. During prolonged cool weather they may become dormant for days on end and, in cold parts of the world, such as northern Europe, they hibernate for several months in order to avoid extreme cold.

Snakes differ from lizards in several respects. No snakes have legs, whereas most lizards do. The few species of lizards that do not have legs, such as the slow-worm and the glass lizards, have eyelids. Snakes do not have eyelids, but most have a transparent scale, called the **brille**, covering their eyes. Snakes also have a single row of specialised scales, the **ventral scales**, running along their undersides, whereas lizards have several rows of scales, arranged in various ways, on their undersides.

Other differences involve the jaws, which in most snakes consist of loosely connected bones that can be stretched to a remarkable degree during swallowing, and several internal characteristics that are the result of their elongated shape.

American glass lizards, *Ophisaurus,* and other legless lizards are sometimes confused with snakes

Amphisbaenians such as *Blanus cinereus* from Spain, superficially resemble earthworms

Size and shape

Snakes vary greatly in size: the smallest are barely 15 cm in length while the largest grow to almost 10 m. Most species, however, including nearly all the European and North American species, are between 1 m and 2 m when adult.

All snakes are long and thin, but some are longer and thinner than others. The shape of a snake is dependent on its lifestyle – tree-dwelling (or arboreal) species tend to be very slender and have long tails that they use to grasp branches (**prehensile**), active ground-dwelling species may also be slender but do not have prehensile tails, while species that lie in wait for their prey are thickset and often have very short tails. Similarly, some snakes have narrow heads that are indistinct from their necks and bodies whereas others have broad, triangular heads.

Snakes, like all reptiles, are covered in **scales**. The shape and number of scales, especially those on the head, are an aid to identification. Most snakes, including all the typical harmless and back-fanged species and the cobras and their relatives, have large, plate-like scales on their heads. Each plate has a special name and snakes of the same species tend to have identical or similar arrangements of these scales. Primitive snakes, and the boas, pythons and vipers, usually have many small, irregular scales covering their heads.

The scales on the body may be smooth and shiny, or they may have a ridge, or **keel**, running along their centre. Like the snake's shape, the type of scale is associated with the snake's habits, so burrowing snakes, for instance, always have smooth shiny scales, whereas snakes that live in swamps and marshes usually have keeled scales, regardless of which families they belong to.

Snakes shed the outer layer of their skin as they grow. Young snakes, which grow quickly, shed more frequently than older snakes, whose growth rate slows down. During shedding, the snake starts by rubbing its snout on a rough object. When the skin on its head has been freed, it pushes through dense vegetation, or over rough ground, and crawls out of its skin, which is left inside out. The discarded skin is transparent, although traces of the markings can sometimes be seen on it. The snake's colours and markings are brighter immediately after it has shed.

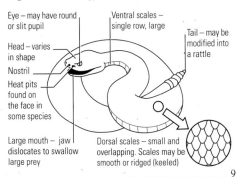

Eye – may have round or slit pupil

Head – varies in shape

Nostril

Heat pits found on the face in some species

Large mouth – jaw dislocates to swallow large prey

Ventral scales – single row, large

Tail – may be modified into a rattle

Dorsal scales – small and overlapping. Scales may be smooth or ridged (keeled)

Senses

Snakes have some of the same senses – sight, smell, etc. – that other animals use, but they have also evolved additional senses, perhaps because their eyesight and hearing are not very good. Snakes use their tongues to pick up scent particles from the atmosphere. First they flick their tongue about in the air and then withdraw it into their mouth. There they insert the tip of each fork into a pair of small chambers in the roof of their mouths: these chambers form the **Jacobson's organ**, which is connected directly to the brain. Although snakes can also smell through their nostrils, the tongue and Jacobson's organ enhance this sense.

Three groups of snakes – the boas, pythons and pit vipers – have an additional sense organ not seen in other animals.

Rattlesnakes use their tongues and their heat pits to investigate their surroundings

Pythons often have a row of heat pits along their lip scales

These are **heat pits**, and are found on the face. Each pit is large and is lined with a sensitive membrane that detects heat. In this way, species with pits can pinpoint the position of warm-blooded animals, which form their main prey, *even in total darkness*. Furthermore, by comparing the 'signals' received by the pits on either side of their heads, they can even judge the distance to their prey and therefore strike accurately.

Boas and pythons have a series of pits, located in the scales bordering the upper and lower lips; boas have the pits between the scales and pythons have them within the scales. In pit vipers, however, there is a single pit on each side of the head, located just below an imaginary line drawn between the eye and the nostril.

Feeding

Snakes' diets greatly depend on their size. They all eat other animals but, as they have no limbs to help them handle and dismember their prey, they must swallow it whole. In order to get around this limitation, their jaws are modified in such a way that they can be dislocated temporarily when swallowing, and their skin is very elastic. By these means, a snake can tackle prey larger than its head. The food of the very largest snakes, then, may include small deer and even crocodiles. Most snakes, however, usually feed on smaller prey, such as mice, rats, frogs, lizards and fish. A surprisingly large number specialise in eating other snakes, which are, of course, the ideal shape to be swallowed!

Pythons always constrict their prey

Snakes can swallow prey larger than their heads

The method of capturing prey takes several forms. Some species, especially those that eat frogs, fish, worms and other small animals, eat their prey live – they just pick it up and begin swallowing. The boas and pythons, as well as many other species, **constrict** their prey, throwing several coils of their body around it and tightening their grip until it cannot breathe: they do not crush their prey, but suffocate it. Snakes from four families have **venom** fangs. These species inject their prey with powerful venoms that kill it quickly and efficiently. In this way the snake avoids the possible risk of injury while it is overpowering its prey.

Defence

Snakes have many enemies and they have several means of preventing themselves from being killed or eaten. The most effective and common method is to avoid detection. Many are well camouflaged so that they blend in to their natural surroundings: tree snakes are green or brown, desert snakes may be yellow or light brown, etc. Others have very intricate markings consisting of blotches, bands or stripes and these are intended to confuse predators by disguising the outline of the snake. Yet other species are brightly coloured, with contrasting bands of red, yellow, white, black and so on. This is to warn or frighten potential enemies, but it may also create an optical illusion: when the snake moves and the bands flicker quickly past, the predator may be confused as to which direction the snake is travelling.

If a snake fails to avoid detection, or if its warning colours do not deter an enemy, it may resort to other means of defence. Many species bite, even though only a few are venomous, and a

Warning coloration in a harmless milk snake

number of them hiss and puff up their bodies in order to appear larger and more fierce than they are. Others form themselves into a ball, with their heads safely tucked away among the coils and they may raise their tail and wave it about as if it is their head. A few play dead by turning over onto their backs and allowing their tongue to hang out of their mouths; this is often accompanied by the secretion of a foul-smelling substance from glands at the base of their tail.

The rattlesnakes have a unique way of warning their enemies: their rattle is formed from parts of old shed skins, which are trapped by a constriction at the end of their tail. Each time the snake sheds its skin a new segment is added and the rattle gets longer (although the end of the rattle may get broken off from time to time). By vibrating its tail, the rattlesnake makes a loud buzzing noise, warning predators that it is dangerous and also alerting large animals, such as cattle, to its presence.

Many snakes are well camouflaged

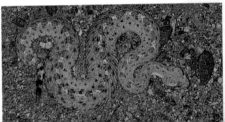

Reproduction

Reproduction is quite varied among snake species. Most lay eggs, which have a pliable shell through which water is absorbed during the development of the embryo. These eggs are laid in a secluded place with a stable temperature and some moisture. Snake eggs can take up to three months to hatch and the female that lays them usually plays no part in their future development. Female pythons, however, brood their eggs by coiling around them throughout the incubation period. They control their temperature by transferring heat from their bodies to the eggs and some species even produce a small amount of heat internally in order to keep the eggs warm. The way in which they do this is not yet understood.

Others species retain their eggs inside their bodies, without shells, until they are at the point of hatching. Their young are fully formed when born. Giving birth to live young is an adaptation to cold environments: by retaining the eggs inside their bodies the females can help the incubation along by basking and keeping their bodies warm. Snakes that lay eggs must rely on the weather to provide enough heat for incubation. Other groups of snakes are live-bearing for other reasons: aquatic snakes, including most of the sea snakes, are unable to lay eggs because they rarely, if ever, come onto the land. Similarly, tree-dwelling species tend to be live-bearing to avoid having to move down to ground level.

A single species of snake, the Brahminy Blind

Snake (p.23) is **parthenogenic** – this means that there are only females of this species. Once they reach breeding size they start to lay eggs without needing to mate with a male. All of the eggs hatch into females.

Young snakes are able to fend for themselves as soon as they hatch or are born. They usually shed their skin within a few days and then search for a suitable place to live and hunt for food. Growth rates vary, but small species may be large enough to breed within one year; medium-sized snakes take two to four years to reach maturity, and large snakes, such as boas and pythons, take at least four years, sometimes longer.

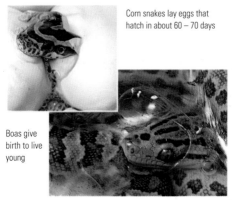

Corn snakes lay eggs that hatch in about 60 – 70 days

Boas give birth to live young

Habitats

Although temperature limits their activity and numbers in countries with cool climates, in tropical regions snakes have moved into many habitats. There are totally aquatic snakes, including sea snakes, snakes that live their entire lives beneath the ground and others that spend much of their time in the upper branches of huge forest trees. Each species is well adapted to its habitat, in shape, colour and behaviour, leading to a much wider variety of size, shape and colour than is generally realised.

Snakes that live in similar habitats often evolve along similar lines so that, even if they are unrelated, they come to look and behave like one another. When two or more snakes come to resemble one another in this way, they are said to have undergone **convergent evolution**.

Hot, dry places are especially rich in snakes. This is Namaqualand, S. Africa, home of the horned adder and many other species

Conservation

Many snakes are becoming increasingly rare. Although many reasons contribute to their decline, habitat destruction is the most important one. Numerous habitats are shrinking, through the activities of agriculture, forestry, urbanisation and road building. Some species are protected, and collecting or disturbing them is illegal. Unfortunately, these measures only protect individual snakes: thousands are killed by road traffic each year and hundreds of thousands die because the places where they live are destroyed or altered. Snakes have an important role to play in the web of life: many do a useful job of controlling the numbers of rodents and other pests and they all have a right to exist.

A harmless mole snake killed by traffic on a S. African road

Identification

Because they are all roughly the same shape, snakes can be difficult for non-specialists to identify. Furthermore, snakes are most often seen when they are moving rapidly away, having been disturbed by the observer. Points to note are the general outline of the snake (slender, medium or stout-bodied), its size (without exaggeration!) and its colour and markings. In many cases, just one or two of these characters will be sufficient if you are in an area where only a few species live. In some tropical countries, however, exact identification is only possible after detailed examination of the specimens, including counting the scales – hardly recommended where venomous species are known to occur! There is no universal way of distinguishing all venomous snakes from all non-venomous ones, although certain groups, such as rattlesnakes, can be identified with relative ease.

Finally, it is worth noting that certain parts of the world are totally lacking in snakes. Ireland, for instance, has no species, although a legless lizard (the slow-worm) occurs there, and there are no snakes in New Zealand. Cold regions, such as Scandinavia and northern Canada have only a small number of species.

Of the eight families grouped together in this section, three contain species that look very similar and the other five each contain only a small number of species. They are thought to have evolved very early in the history of snakes. They all have a **pelvic girdle** (the bone to which their hind limbs would be attached if they had them) and some have small thorn-like structures, the remains of hind limbs that have all but disappeared.

Primitive burrowing snakes (blind and thread snakes) The three families of primitive burrowing snakes are the Anomalepididae (which has no English name), the thread snakes (Leptotyphlopidae) and the blind snakes (Typhlopidae). All the 260 or so species in these families are small, from about 10–95 cm in length. They have thin, cylindrical bodies, short tails and smooth, shiny scales. Their eyes are minuscule and their jaws are more rigid than in other snakes. They are found in most of the warmer parts of the world.

Primitive specialised snakes Of the five other families of primitive snakes, the file snake family (Acrochordidae) contains three species, all of which are aquatic. The sunbeam snake family (Xenopeltidae) has two species, and two further families contain only a single species: the Mexican burrowing snake (Loxocemidae) and the South American pipe snake (Aniliidae). The family of shield-tailed snakes and Asian pipe snakes (Uropeltidae) from India, Sri Lanka and South-east Asia contains about 55 species, but these are all very similar.

WESTERN BLIND SNAKE *Leptotyphlops humilis*

A slender, silvery pink snake with a blunt head and tail. The eyes are barely visible beneath the scales on the head. It can easily be mistaken for an earthworm.

Size	To about 30 cm.
Distribution	SW USA and NW Mexico.
Habitat	Deserts and other dry habitats with soil suitable for burrowing. Only seen on the surface at night.
Food	Small insects, including ants and termites.
Breeding	Lays 2–6 eggs in late summer.
Notes	The only other species in North America is the Texas Thread Snake, *L. dulcis*, which is very similar in appearance, but has a more eastern distribution.

BRAHMINY BLIND SNAKE *Ramphotyphlops braminus*

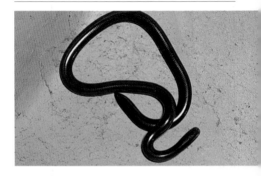

A very slender, brown snake with a small spine on the tip of the tail. Its scales are shiny and the eyes are covered by scales. It looks very similar to a number of other related worm snakes.

Size	To about 15 cm.
Distribution	Native to India, Sri Lanka and South-east Asia, but accidentally introduced into South Africa, Australia, Mexico, Hawaii and Florida.
Habitat	Damp soil in forests, fields, etc. Often under stones and pieces of debris.
Food	Small insects and earthworms.
Breeding	Egg-laying. This species is parthenogenic (see p.17).
Notes	The only member of its family in many places. Elsewhere, close examination is necessary for positive identification.

EUROPEAN WORM SNAKE *Typhlops vermicularis*

A slender pinkish-brown or yellowish-brown snake, slightly paler underneath. There may be a small dark spot on each scale on the upper surface. Very earthworm-like.

Size	To about 35 cm.
Distribution	SE Europe, Turkey, the Middle East and parts of W Asia.
Habitat	Dry sandy soil, often under rocks.
Food	Small insects, including ants and their pupae.
Breeding	Egg-laying, with clutches of about 6 eggs laid in early summer.
Notes	The only blind snake in Europe. Elsewhere, it is easily confused with other species.

ARAFURA FILE SNAKE *Acrochordus arafurae*

All file snakes are large and ungainly, with very rough skins. They are completely aquatic and never come out of the water voluntarily. This large species is brown with faint light and dark markings.

Size	Females to about 160 cm, males about half this length.
Distribution	N Australia.
Habitat	Freshwater rivers, lakes and billabongs.
Food	Fish.
Breeding	Live-bearing, with litters of 11–27 young, born underwater. Takes many years to mature.
Notes	The only freshwater file snake in Australia.

SMALL FILE SNAKE *Acrochordus granulatus*

A typical file snake with a stout body, rough skin and small eyes. The young are boldly banded in black and white, but the markings fade as they grow.

Size	To about 120 cm.
Distribution	Coastal waters from W India through South-east Asia and the Philippines to N Australia.
Habitat	Estuaries, river mouths, mangrove swamps and coastal waters.
Food	Fish, crustaceans and snails.
Breeding	Live-bearing.
Notes	The third member of the family is the Javan File Snake, *A. javanicus*, a large grey species found in South-east Asia.

SUNBEAM SNAKE *Xenopeltis unicolor*

A beautiful shiny snake with smooth, iridescent scales. Its head is flattened from top to bottom and it has tiny round eyes. Its snout is shovel-shaped, for burrowing. The upperside is dark grey and the underside is lighter, almost white.

Size	To just over 100 cm.
Distribution	South-east Asia.
Habitat	Open forests, agricultural areas and parks; usually under debris.
Food	Frogs, lizards, other snakes and small rodents.
Breeding	Egg-laying, with clutches of about 6 eggs.
Notes	The only other sunbeam snake, *X. hainanensis*, comes from China, and was only discovered recently.

MEXICAN BURROWING SNAKE *Loxocemus bicolor*

This snake is the only member of its family, although it used to be grouped with the pythons. It is superficially similar to the Sunbeam Snake (p.27), but the body is more rounded and the scales are smaller and slightly less iridescent. Irregular patches of white scales sometimes develop on the body.

Size	To about 130 cm.
Distribution	W Mexico and neighbouring parts of Central America.
Habitat	Tropical dry or moist forests.
Food	Other reptiles and their eggs, small mammals.
Breeding	Egg-laying.
Notes	A rare species with no other similar snakes in its region.

SOUTH AMERICAN PIPE SNAKE *Anilius scytale*

A brightly banded snake with rings of black and red (or orange). It has a cylindrical body, smooth scales and small eyes. Like other brightly banded snakes, this species is sometimes known as the 'false coral snake' because of its similarity to the venomous coral snakes (pp.191-194).

Size	To about 120 cm, but usually smaller.
Distribution	N South America.
Habitat	Rain forests.
Food	Probably other reptiles.
Breeding	Egg-laying.
Notes	This snake is quite rare and its natural history is poorly known.

ASIAN PIPE SNAKE *Cylindrophis rufus*

A small black or brown snake with narrow bands of white or cream. When threatened it lifts its tail off the ground and waves it about. This shows off the bright red, black and white underside, and is thought to keep predators away.

Size	To about 90 cm.
Distribution	India, Sri Lanka and South-east Asia.
Habitat	Forests and agricultural areas, especially with damp soil.
Food	Reptiles, including smaller snakes, and possibly insects and their larvae.
Breeding	Live-bearing.
Notes	There are several other species of pipe snakes in Asia, all of which are rather similar in appearance, but this is the most common.

PRIMITIVE 'BOAS'

The snakes belonging to the following two families – the Wood Snakes or West Indian Boas (Tropidophiidae) and the Round Island Boas (Bolyeriidae) – are not, strictly speaking, boas at all. They were classified with the boas for many years, however, and have certain similarities with them: they all have remains of hind limbs, in the form of small spurs, their heads are covered with numerous small scales, and they all constrict their prey.

The **Tropidophiidae** is a family of 21 species. Most are found in the West Indies, especially on the island of Cuba, but a few occur on the Central or South American mainland. They are small boa-like snakes that live secretive lives, emerging mainly at night to feed. Several species are rare; some are known from only two or three specimens.

The **Bolyeriidae** contains just two species, one of which, the Round Island keeled-scaled boa, is probably extinct. The other species also lives on Round Island, near Mauritius in the Indian Ocean, and is endangered. Much of the habitat on Round Island was destroyed after the introduction of goats and rabbits in the nineteenth century, and introduced rats preyed on the snakes' eggs and young.

HAITIAN WOOD SNAKE *Tropidophis haitianus*

A slender snake with smooth scales. This variable species has different colour forms on different islands. It may be brown, olive, tan or orange, with several rows of small darker blotches running down the back.

Size	To about 70 cm.
Distribution	Cuba, Hispaniola (Haiti and Dominican Republic) and Jamaica.
Habitat	Forests, scrub and rocky places. Sometimes in bromeliads (air plants) several metres above the ground.
Food	Frogs, lizards and small rodents.
Breeding	Live-bearing, with litters of about 8 young.
Notes	The only species of *Tropidophis* on Haiti and Jamaica. Several similar species are found on Cuba.

CUBAN WOOD SNAKE *Tropidophis melanurus*

A highly variable species with several colour forms. The most common form is brown with darker blotches along the back. The orange form, shown here, is one of the more brightly coloured ones. The tip of the tail is yellow and may be used to lure small animals, such as frogs and lizards, within range.

Size	To 1 m, but some forms are much smaller.
Distribution	Cuba.
Habitat	Forests, gardens, etc., usually under logs and other debris.
Food	Frogs, lizards, birds and small rodents.
Breeding	Live-bearing, with litters of up to 10 young.
Notes	Some forms are easily confused with other species of *Tropidophis*, 9 of which live on Cuba, but the orange form is unmistakable.

BANANA BOA *Ungaliophis continentalis*

A small, well-built snake with smooth scales. It is light greyish-brown, with darker ovals along the back, each surrounded by a light-coloured border. The top of the head is black. It is known as the Banana Boa because it sometimes turns up in shipments of bananas.

Size	To about 50 cm.
Distribution	Central America.
Habitat	Tropical forests, often in trees or bromeliad plants.
Food	Frogs, lizards, birds and small mammals.
Breeding	Live-bearing, with litters of 1–6 young.
Notes	A related species, *U. panamensis*, is similar in appearance, but is rarer and its natural history is poorly known.

ROUND ISLAND BOA *Casarea dussumieri*

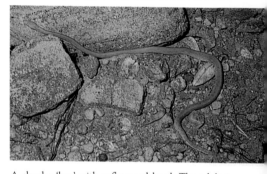

A slender 'boa' with a flattened head. The adult is dark grey with some paler markings on its sides and the juvenile is brown or olive. This species is extremely rare and can only be seen on Round Island and at the Jersey Wildlife Preservation Trust, where it is bred in captivity.

Size	To about 1 m.
Distribution	Round Island, in the Indian Ocean.
Habitat	Rocky places, among leaf-litter and in crevices.
Food	Lizards.
Breeding	Egg-laying, with clutches of 3 to 10 eggs.
Notes	This snake cannot be confused with any other.

BOAS AND PYTHONS (BOIDAE)

The boas and pythons are well-known snakes, found in most tropical countries. Many are very large (the six largest snakes belong to this family), but others are small or moderate in size. Boas and pythons have the remains of hind limbs, in the form of spurs, which are often more prominent in males. Pythons' heads are covered with irregular scales that are larger than those on their bodies, whereas most boas' heads are covered with numerous small scales. They also differ in their reproduction: pythons lay eggs, which the female broods, whereas boas give birth to live young.

They are all powerful constrictors and feed on mammals, birds and reptiles. The larger species can even tackle small antelope and domestic animals such as goats and pigs. There have been cases of attacks on humans, but these are very rare. Boas and pythons are found in a variety of habitats, and the family includes burrowing, terrestrial and arboreal (tree-dwelling) species. They may be active by day or night.

Many pythons and boas have heat-sensitive pits on their upper and lower jaws; these may be positioned between the scales or within them (see pp.10–11). However, some species do not have pits at all, such as the Common Boa, *Boa constrictor*.

Many boas and pythons are economically important because they eat large numbers of pest species, especially rodents. Several of them are rare in the wild, due to habitat destruction, wanton killing because of prejudice, and collecting for the pet trade. Therefore, all species now have some degree of international protection.

DUMERIL'S BOA *Acrantophis dumerili*

A thickset boa with beautiful, complex markings of dark brown on a tan or fawn background. It has a dark brown line passing through the eye and inky black marks on the upper lips. The young often have a pinkish tinge. It lacks heat pits.

Size To about 1.5 m.

Distribution Madagascar.

Habitat Forests, especially near streams and rivers; mainly on the ground among leaves.

Food Small mammals and birds.

Breeding Live-bearing, with litters of up to 20 young.

Notes The other Madagascan ground boa, *A. madagascariensis*, is slightly larger and its dark markings are less extensive. Both species are sometimes referred to the genus *Boa*, and both are strictly protected.

COMMON BOA *Boa constrictor*

A large boa (though not as large as is often thought!) with quite variable markings: usually grey or beige with dark brown markings along the back. It has a dark line on the top of the head and another dark line runs through each eye. It lacks heat pits.

Size	To about 4 m, usually rather less.
Distribution	South and Central America, including some West Indian islands (Dominica, Trinidad, St Lucia).
Habitat	Rain forest clearings and riversides, agricultural land and thorn scrub. Often around villages.
Food	Mammals and birds.
Breeding	Live-bearing, with litters of up to 50 young.
Notes	The most common boa and not easily mistaken for other species. A common exhibit in zoos and a popular pet.

PACIFIC GROUND BOA *Candoia aspera*

A small, chunky boa with tiny scales covering the top of the head. Its markings, broad brown bands on a darker background, are sometimes obscure. It lacks heat pits.

Size	To about 75 cm.
Distribution	New Guinea and nearby islands.
Habitat	Forests, especially near rivers.
Food	Frogs, lizards and small mammals.
Breeding	Live-bearing, with litters of about 10 young.
Notes	This snake is sometimes known as the 'viper boa' because it bears a superficial resemblance to the Death Adder (p.183), which is also found on New Guinea.

PACIFIC BOA *Candoia carinata*

Usually a thickset species, but sometimes more slender. It may be light grey, almost white, with a broad, irregular, dark line running along the back, or brick-red with a maroon line. The head is flattened from top to bottom and it has an obliquely angled snout. It lacks heat pits.

Size	To about 1.5 m.
Distribution	New Guinea and nearby islands, including the Solomon Islands.
Habitat	Forests.
Food	Lizards, birds and small mammals.
Breeding	Live-bearing, with litters of up to 70 very small young.
Notes	A highly variable species; its shape and colour depend largely on which island it comes from.

RUBBER BOA *Charina bottae*

A thick, cylindrical snake that is uniform brown or olive. Its scales are small and shiny and the eyes are also small. It has a short, blunt tail, which it sometimes raises off the ground and uses to make mock 'strikes' in order to deflect attack away from its head. It lacks heat pits.

Size	50–80 cm.
Distribution	W North America.
Habitat	Grassland, scrub and pinewoods; usually beneath logs and bark, etc.
Food	Small salamanders, snakes, birds and small rodents.
Breeding	Live-bearing, with litters of 2–8 young.
Notes	A slow-moving snake that never attempts to bite. Look for the tiny scales and 'rubbery' appearance.

EMERALD TREE BOA *Corallus caninus*

A beautiful boa with a strong resemblance to the Green Tree Python (p.58), an example of convergent evolution (see p.18). Juveniles are red or orange, but their colour changes to green during the first year. It has a row of white markings along the back and large, prominent heat pits.

Size	To about 1.6 m.
Distribution	Amazon Basin (South America).
Habitat	Tropical rain forests, but only in large trees.
Food	Birds and small mammals.
Breeding	Live-bearing, with litters of up to 20 young.
Notes	The only species with which it can be confused is the Green Tree Python from Australasia.

AMAZON TREE BOA *Corallus enhydris*

A slender tree snake varying between brown, yellow, orange and grey. Some have darker markings on the back, but others are plain. The young are more brightly coloured than the adults. It has prominent heat pits.

Size	To about 1.8 m.
Distribution	South America, including the Amazon Basin, and into Central America. Also several West Indian islands (Trinidad, Tobago, The Grenadines, St Vincent and Grenada).
Habitat	Forests with tall trees.
Food	Lizards, frogs, birds and small mammals.
Breeding	Live-bearing, with litters of 10–20 young.
Notes	Various colour forms can be produced in a single litter, but the long, slender shape, large eyes and heat pits make this snake easy to identify.

43

CUBAN BOA _Epicrates angulifer_

The Cuban Boa may be tan, yellowish or brown, with a pattern of dark angular markings on a lighter background. These markings are difficult to see on some specimens. It has heat pits.

Size	To nearly 4 m.
Distribution	Cuba.
Habitat	Forests, where it frequently climbs into trees, and caves.
Food	Mammals (bats and rodents) and birds, including domestic chickens.
Breeding	Live-bearing, with small litters of large young.
Notes	The only large boa on Cuba. Although once common, this species is declining as a result of forest clearance and sugar cane cultivation.

BRAZILIAN RAINBOW BOA *Epicrates cenchria cenchria*

There are nine subspecies of rainbow boa of which this is one of the most colourful. Its scales are very glossy with a beautiful iridescent sheen, hence its name. A row of irregular black circles runs down the back and there are additional black 'eyespots' along each side. It has shallow heat pits.

Size	To about 2 m, but usually smaller.
Distribution	N South America.
Habitat	Tropical forests and forest clearings.
Food	Birds and small mammals.
Breeding	Live-bearing, with litters of up to 30 young.
Notes	One of the more distinctive rainbow boas; its bright orange coloration distinguishes it from the others.

ARGENTINE RAINBOW BOA *Epicrates cenchria alvarezi*

This form of rainbow boa is very distinctive, being marked in shades of brown, grey and/or tan. Its flanks are grey with brown markings and the centre of the back is brown with pale circles. It has shallow heat pits.

Size	To about 1.2 m.
Distribution	Argentina.
Habitat	Forests.
Food	Birds and small mammals.
Breeding	Live-bearing, with litters of 5–14 young.
Notes	Other forms of rainbow boa are intermediate in appearance between this subspecies and the Brazilian Rainbow Boa (p.45).

HAITIAN BOA *Epicrates striatus*

A highly variable species with a series of large blotches along the back, some of which may be joined together. These blotches may be dark grey, brown or reddish and the background is lighter, usually pale grey. It has shallow heat pits.

Size	To about 2.3 m.
Distribution	Haiti and nearby islands, and the Bahamas.
Habitat	Forests, including pinewoods and mangroves. Likes to climb and has been found in thatched roofs.
Food	Young eat lizards and adults eat birds, including domestic chickens, and small mammals.
Breeding	Live-bearing, with litters of up to 50 very small young.
Notes	The only large boa on Haiti or the Bahamas, although there are smaller species.

AFRICAN SAND BOA *Eryx colubrinus*

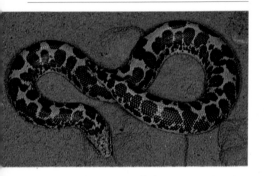

All the sand boas are small, burrowing snakes that bear little resemblance to the larger members of their family. This species is cream, yellow or orange with large blotches of light or dark brown along the back. It has a short tail, rounded snout and small eyes. It lacks heat pits.

Size	To about 80 cm. Females are usually larger than males.
Distribution	NE and E Africa.
Habitat	Arid, semi-desert regions.
Food	Small mammals.
Breeding	Live-bearing, with litters of 5–12 young.
Notes	Specimens from Kenya (subspecies *loveridgei*) are more brightly coloured than those from other areas.

ROUGH-SCALED SAND BOA *Eryx conicus*

A heavily built snake that is cream or sandy with a series of dark brown blotches along the back. These may join together to form an irregular zigzag pattern. There are smaller brown blotches on the flanks.

Size	To 1 m.
Distribution	Pakistan, India and Sri Lanka.
Habitat	Dry, sandy areas (and more humid areas in a few places).
Food	Rodents and, occasionally, birds and lizards.
Breeding	Live-bearing, with litters of up to 11 young.
Notes	The only sand boa in the region. Although normally slow-moving, it can bite suddenly with a sideways swipe of the head.

JAVELIN SAND BOA *Eryx jaculus*

A stout snake with a short blunt tail. It is pale yellow, buff or grey with irregular darker markings along the back, which may be spots or bars and are usually connected to form a net-like pattern. It has a dark line running from the eye to the corner of the jaw. It lacks heat pits.

Size	To 80 cm, but usually less. Males are smaller than females.
Distribution	SE Europe, Turkey and parts of the Middle East.
Habitat	Dry, sandy places; usually under rocks.
Food	Rodents, but also small birds and lizards.
Breeding	Live-bearing, with litters of up to 20 young.
Notes	The only member of the boa family in Europe. Elsewhere its range overlaps with two other small Asian species, *E. tataricus* and *E. miliaris*.

GREEN ANACONDA *Eunectes murinus*

The world's largest snake. Despite its name, it is olive, brown or greenish-yellow, with regular dark ovals on the back and black and yellow 'eyespots' along the sides. It has a small head and its eyes point upwards, an adaptation to its aquatic lifestyle. It lacks heat pits.

Size	To 10 m, but usually much smaller. There are reports of gigantic anacondas of 62 feet (19 m) from eighteenth-century explorers, but these are almost certainly exaggerated.
Distribution	Tropical South America, including Trinidad.
Habitat	Swamps.
Food	Large reptiles, birds and mammals; including alligators and freshwater turtles.
Breeding	Live-bearing, with large litters of young.
Notes	Adults unmistakable due to size. Often aggressive.

YELLOW ANACONDA *Eunectes notaeus*

A yellowish snake with an attractive pattern of large black blotches or saddles along the back. It has additional dark markings on the flanks. Like the Green Anaconda (p.51), the eyes point upwards. It lacks heat pits.

Size	To about 2 m.
Distribution	N South America.
Habitat	Swamps.
Food	Reptiles, birds and mammals.
Breeding	Live-bearing, with large litters.
Notes	Often in zoos and reptile parks. Usually aggressive.

MEXICAN ROSY BOA *Lichanura trivirgata trivirgata*

A heavy-bodied snake with a narrow head and blunt tail. It has wide stripes of dark brown running the length of the body on a pale grey or buff background. The stripes may be very well defined or they may be ragged. It lacks heat pits.

Size	To about 1 m or slightly more.
Distribution	NW Mexico (Sonora, Baja California Sur); just into S Arizona, USA.
Habitat	Rocky outcrops, scrub and semi-desert areas. A good climber.
Food	Small birds and mammals.
Breeding	Live-bearing, with litters of 3–5 young (occasionally up to 10).
Notes	A slow-moving, gentle snake that rarely bites and makes a good pet.

BAJA CALIFORNIAN ROSY BOA *Lichanura trivirgata saslowi*

Similar in build to the Mexican Rosy Boa (p.53), but the stripes of this subspecies are orange or brownish-orange and are usually very well defined. Its eyes are also orange. It lacks heat pits.

Size	To about 1 m.
Distribution	Mexico (central Baja California).
Habitat	Rocky outcrops and lava flows.
Food	Small mammals and birds.
Breeding	Live-bearing, with litters of 3–8 young.
Notes	The most brightly coloured form of rosy boa. Other forms include one from Arizona (*L. t. myriolepis*) with uneven brown stripes, and a uniform brown one (*L. t. roseofusca*) from S California.

MADAGASCAN TREE BOA *Sanzinia madagascariensis*

A green or greenish-brown tree boa with a broad head and long, prehensile tail. It is marked with dark bands or blotches, each edged in white. Juveniles are reddish-brown with similar markings. It has prominent heat pits.

Size	To 1.5 m.
Distribution	Madagascar.
Habitat	Forested areas, where it lives mostly in trees.
Food	Mammals and birds.
Breeding	Live-bearing, with litters of 3–16 young.
Notes	Once widespread and common, its future is threatened by habitat destruction. It is the only large tree-dwelling snake in Madagascar.

BLACK-HEADED PYTHON *Aspidites melanocephalus*

A fairly slender python with a distinctive glossy black head and neck. The rest of the body is yellowish, buff or pinkish-brown with darker crossbars. The crossbars are wider at the centre of the back than on the flanks and may join together along the midline. It has no heat pits.

Size	To 2.6 m.
Distribution	The N half of Australia.
Habitat	Tropical and subtropical grasslands and hills. Usually in hollow trees, caves and crevices.
Food	Snakes, small mammals and ground-nesting birds.
Breeding	Egg-laying, with clutches of 5–10 eggs. Female coils around eggs until they hatch.
Notes	The only similar species is the Woma, *A. ramsayi*, which lacks the black head and neck.

CALABAR GROUND PYTHON *Calabaria reinhardtii*

This unusual python has a cylindrical body and a blunt snout and tail. It is patterned with irregular patches of black and brown, orange or red scales. When it is threatened it hides its head and raises its tail, which acts as a false head. It has no heat pits.

Size	To about 1 m.
Distribution	W Africa.
Habitat	Forests and riversides, in leaf-litter and burrows that it digs for itself.
Food	Small mammals.
Breeding	Egg-laying, with clutches of 2–5 proportionately large eggs.
Notes	Unmistakable: there are no other similar species.

GREEN TREE PYTHON *Chondropython viridis*

A bright green tree snake with a long, prehensile tail and a broad head. There is usually a row of small white spots along the back. Juveniles are bright sulphur yellow or red, but change to green by the time they are two years old. It has very prominent heat pits.

Size	To 1.5 m, sometimes more.
Distribution	New Guinea and nearby islands, and the very N tip of Queensland, Australia.
Habitat	Rain forests. Completely arboreal.
Food	Birds and mammals, including bats. Young may also eat lizards and tree frogs.
Breeding	Egg-laying, with clutches of up to 26 eggs laid in a tree cavity. Female coils around eggs until they hatch.
Notes	Could be confused with its distant relative, the Emerald Tree Boa (p.42).

WHITE-LIPPED PYTHON *Liasis albertisii*

An elegant python with an elongated body and narrow head. The body is bronze and iridescent. The head may be the same colour or (more commonly) black with a row of black-edged, white scales bordering the mouth. It has prominent heat pits.

Size	To 2.4 m.
Distribution	New Guinea and neighbouring islands.
Habitat	Lowland rain forest and swamps.
Food	Small mammals and birds.
Breeding	Egg-laying, with clutches of 9–18 eggs. Female coils around eggs until they hatch.
Notes	Usually aggressive.

CHILDREN'S PYTHON *Liasis childreni*

One of the smaller pythons, with a slender body and narrow head. It is light brown, fading to white below. The young have blotches of darker brown on their backs and sides. This species has large scales covering the top of the head and heat pits in the upper and lower lip scales. The one above is brooding eggs.

Size	To 1 m.
Distribution	N Australia.
Habitat	Plains and hills, often near rock outcrops and light woodland.
Food	Small mammals, including bats, frogs and lizards.
Breeding	Egg-laying, with clutches of 8–16 eggs. Female coils around eggs until they hatch.
Notes	The Pygmy Python, *L. perthensis*, is very similar, but even smaller (to 54 cm) and reddish-brown.

MACKLOT'S PYTHON *Liasis mackloti*

A very slender python with a narrow head and smooth, iridescent scales. It is olive to brown and irregularly speckled with small groups of black scales. Its lower lips are white and it has heat pits. This picture is of the Savu Island subspecies, *L.m.savuensis*.

Size	To about 2 m or slightly more.
Distribution	New Guinea and some nearby islands.
Habitat	Coastal forests.
Food	Birds and small mammals; perhaps also other snakes and lizards.
Breeding	Egg-laying, with clutches of up to 20 eggs.
Notes	Similar to the Australian Water Python, *L. fuscus*, which is thought to be the same species by some experts.

SPOTTED PYTHON *Liasis maculosus*

A small python, similar to the Children's Python (p.60), but boldly marked with large dark brown blotches on a pale brown or yellowish background. It has large scales covering the head and heat pits in the scales of the upper and lower jaws.

Size	To 1.35 m.
Distribution	NE Australia.
Habitat	Grassland, rocky outcrops and lightly wooded areas; in caves and hollow trees.
Food	Small mammals, including bats, birds and lizards.
Breeding	Egg-laying, with clutches of 4–16 eggs. Female coils around eggs until they hatch.
Notes	The only other small, blotched python in Australia is Stimson's Python, *L. stimsoni*, which has a paler pattern and is often reddish.

PAPUAN PYTHON *Liasis papuanus*

A large python with a deep head. It is uniform olive-brown or greyish-brown above, pale yellowish-white below. The head is covered with fine speckles of dark grey and the inside of the mouth is black. It has heat pits in a few of the scales of the upper and lower lips.

Size	To about 4 m.
Distribution	New Guinea.
Habitat	Tropical grassland.
Food	Mammals and birds.
Breeding	Egg-laying.
Notes	The natural history of this rare species is poorly known.

AMETHYSTINE (OR SCRUB) PYTHON *Morelia amethistina*

A long, slender species with large scales covering the top of the head. It is brown or yellowish-brown with irregular dark angular markings down the back. It usually has a pale line along each side, at least on the front half of the body. It is Australia's largest snake.

Size	Occasionally to 8.5 m, but usually much less.
Distribution	Extreme NE Australia (Queensland) and New Guinea.
Habitat	Tropical lowland forests and occasionally drier wooded areas.
Food	Mammals, e.g. fruit bats, wallabies, etc., and birds.
Breeding	Egg-laying, with clutches of 7–20 eggs.
Notes	The similar Oenpelli Python, *M. oenpelliensis*, found further west in Arnhemland, N Australia, reaches a similar size but is pale greyish-brown. It lives in rocky places, sheltering in caves and crevices.

DIAMOND PYTHON *Morelia spilota spilota*

A handsome snake that is usually black with a white spot on almost every scale. Some patches of scales may be completely black or white, forming a pattern of spots on the back and stripes on the flanks. It has heat pits in the scales around the mouth.

Size	To 2 m or slightly more.
Distribution	New South Wales, Australia.
Habitat	Woodlands and rocky outcrops. Sometimes around human dwellings, where it is often tolerated because it eats rats.
Food	Mammals and birds.
Breeding	Egg-laying, with clutches of up to 50 eggs.
Notes	The most distinctive form of the Carpet Python (see next page, where other forms are described).

CARPET PYTHON *Morelia spilota variegata*

A widespread and highly variable snake. Typically brown or grey with paler bands crossing the body, which often break up into irregular blotches and streaks. Some Queensland specimens are darker, almost black, with yellow bands.

Size	To 4 m, but usually much less.
Distribution	E and SW Australia; parts of New Guinea.
Habitat	Forests, scrub and rock outcrops. Often along river courses and around human dwellings.
Food	Mammals, including bats, wallabies and other small marsupials, and birds. Young also eat lizards.
Breeding	Egg-laying, with clutches of up to 50 eggs.
Notes	Centralian Carpet Python, *M. bredli*, comes from central Australia, and Rough-scaled Carpet Python, *M. carinata*, from NW Australia.

BLOOD PYTHON *Python curtus*

A short, fat python with complicated and variable markings. The back is brown, with lighter and darker blotches. The flanks are tan with pale grey blotches. In some forms, the brown is replaced with blood red. It has large heat pits.

Size	To 2 m.
Distribution	South-east Asia (Malaysian peninsula, Borneo, Sumatra).
Habitat	Tropical forests.
Food	Mammals and birds, which it ambushes.
Breeding	Egg-laying, with clutches of up to about 20 eggs which the female broods.
Notes	Unmistakable because of its shape, but note colour variation. Borneo forms are brown, Sumatran reddish, but mainland forms can be brown, red or yellowish.

BURMESE PYTHON *Python molurus bivittatus*

A large python with very attractive markings. The underlying colour is yellowish and over this are large interlocking blotches of rich chestnut brown. It has an arrow-shaped dark mark on the top of its head and another dark streak through each eye. It has heat pits.

Size	To 7 m, usually less.
Distribution	India, Sri Lanka, Burma and N Thailand.
Habitat	Tropical forests, fields and around villages.
Food	Mammals and birds.
Breeding	Egg-laying, with clutches of up to about 70 eggs. Female coils around the eggs and may warm them by producing heat internally.
Notes	The Burmese subspecies is the most common in captivity. Specimens from India (*P. m. molurus*) and Sri Lanka (*P. m. pimbura*), are paler overall.

BURMESE PYTHON *Python molurus bivittatus* (albino)

This albino form of the Burmese Python (opposite) is frequently bred in captivity and is often known as the 'golden python'. The dark blotches on the back are yellow while the background is white. The eyes are pinkish. In all other respects, it resembles the normal form of Burmese Python.

Size	Potentially to 7 m, but usually about 4 m.
Distribution	As for Burmese Python.
Habitat	As for Burmese Python. Extremely rare in the wild.
Food	As for Burmese Python.
Breeding	As for Burmese Python.
Notes	Albinos occasionally occur in snake populations and, if they are not eaten by predators, may pass their genes to their offspring. Selective breeding in captivity can produce pure albino strains.

ROYAL (OR BALL) PYTHON *Python regius*

A stocky python with a very dark brown background, and tan, pale brown or yellowish-brown oval blotches on the back. There is another series of light-coloured blotches running along each flank. It has heat pits.

Size	To about 1.5 m.
Distribution	W Africa.
Habitat	Grasslands and river courses.
Food	Small mammals and birds.
Breeding	Egg-laying, with clutches of up to 10 large eggs. Female coils around eggs until they hatch.
Notes	There is one other short, thick python from Africa, the Angolan Python, *P. anchietae*. This very rare species is chocolate-brown with spots and crossbars of cream.

RETICULATED PYTHON *Python reticulatus*

Perhaps the world's longest snake, though not as heavy as the Green Anaconda (p.51). It has intricate markings of black diamonds, edged with yellow, on a grey background. There are irregular white patches along the flanks. It has heat pits.

Size	To 10 m, but usually less.
Distribution	South-east Asia.
Habitat	Tropical forests and clearings, including agricultural areas, villages and even large towns.
Food	Mammals and birds, including domestic livestock.
Breeding	Egg-laying, with some clutches containing nearly 100 eggs. Female coils around eggs.
Notes	A frequent exhibit in zoos, though not as common in captivity as the Burmese Python (p.68), which is more manageable.

African Python *Python sebae*

A muscular python with a wide head covered in numerous small scales. Brown or greenish-brown with an irregular row of dark brown markings and blotches along the back and smaller blotches on the flanks. It has heat pits. The one in the photograph is constricting a Nile Crocodile.

Size	To 5 m or slightly more.
Distribution	Africa, S of the Sahara.
Habitat	Grasslands, especially in rock outcrops and around villages and farms. Often near water.
Food	Mammals and birds; also crocodiles and even fish.
Breeding	Egg-laying, with clutches of about 50 eggs (exceptionally up to 100), which the female coils around until they hatch.
Notes	The only large python in Africa.

Typical Harmless and Back-Fanged Snakes

The **colubrid** family is by far the largest, containing about 1,500 of the 2,500 species of snakes. The family contains many species that are common and widespread, as well as a number of more specialised, rarer species. Most colubrids measure between 50 cm and 2 m, although there are several that fall outside this range. They also vary greatly in shape, colour and markings, depending, to a large extent, on their habits and habitats. Colubrids occupy a great number of ecological 'niches' and there are burrowing, terrestrial, tree-dwelling and aquatic species in the family. The oceans are just about the only habitat to which they have failed to adapt, although there are species living in mangrove swamps and estuaries. Similarly, they prey on a wide range of animals, from worms, insects and other invertebrates, up to medium-sized birds and mammals.

Although the majority of species are completely harmless, some have a Duvernoy's gland, which secretes proteins in the form of a mild venom that is used to subdue and digest prey. These species often have long, sharp fangs at the rear of their upper jaws in order to penetrate the skin of their prey and allow the venom to enter the body and take effect. Most back-fanged colubrids are harmless to humans, but a few, such as the Boomslang (p.98) and the Twig Snake (p.177), both African, produce very toxic secretions that can cause localised pain and even death.

With very few exceptions, the heads of colubrid snakes are covered with large plate-like scales, and the scales on their body may be smooth or keeled.

Identification can be difficult in some parts of the world where numerous similar species live in the same area.

LONG-NOSED TREE SNAKE *Ahaetulla nasuta*

An extremely slender snake: even its head is elongated, with a characteristic pointed snout. The large eyes have horizontal pupils, found only in a few other tree snakes, allowing the snake to judge distances accurately. The green coloration, coupled to the vine-like shape, provides excellent camouflage.

Size	To 2 m, but exceedingly thin.
Distribution	South-east Asia.
Habitat	Trees and bushes in tropical forests.
Food	Mainly lizards, also frogs and small mammals.
Breeding	Live-bearing, with small litters of young.
Notes	The 7 other species of *Ahaetulla* are all similar in appearance. They are all rear-fanged snakes that are probably not dangerous to humans.

ASIAN SLUG-EATING SNAKE *Aplopeltura boa*

A very slender snake with large scales, a deep head, blunt snout and large eyes. It is brown with darker brown crossbars and blotches. Its head has rust-brown markings on the top.

Size	To about 75 cm.
Distribution	South-east Asia.
Habitat	Forests, where it lives in trees. Active only at night.
Food	Slugs and snails.
Breeding	Not known, but thought to lay eggs.
Notes	Specialises in eating slugs and snails and has similar modifications to slug-eating snakes of South America. It is the only member of its genus.

GLOSSY SNAKE *Arizona elegans*

A moderately slender snake with an almost cylindrical body and smooth, shiny scales. The markings are pale brown or grey saddles on a pale tan, cream or brown background. They are very docile and make no attempt to bite, even when first captured.

Size	About 1.5 m.
Distribution	S USA and adjacent parts of Mexico.
Habitat	Dry, open areas, including grassland, scrub, open woods and deserts.
Food	Lizards, snakes and small mammals. A powerful constrictor.
Breeding	Egg-laying, with clutches of up to 20 eggs.
Notes	Similar to gopher and bull snakes (pp.152-154), but the Glossy Snake has smooth scales. Some subspecies are recognised, but their differences are slight.

TRANS-PECOS RATSNAKE *Bogertophis subocularis*

An elegant ratsnake with a slender body, narrow head and large eyes. It ranges from tan, buff or cream to pale yellow, and is marked with dark H-shaped saddles along the back. Its scales are weakly keeled.

Size	To 1.6 m.
Distribution	Chihuahuan Desert (S Texas, S New Mexico and adjacent parts of Mexico).
Habitat	Deserts and semi-arid places, especially where there are rocks. Active only at night.
Food	Small mammals, birds and lizards, which it kills by constriction.
Breeding	Egg-laying; clutches of 3–10 eggs laid in late summer.
Notes	There is also a pale, or 'blonde', form (shown above), with smaller, more rounded, lighter coloured dorsal blotches.

MANGROVE SNAKE *Boiga dendrophila*

A strikingly marked snake, with large glossy scales, yellow lip scales and bold yellow bands on a jet black background. The bands become narrower towards the middle of the back and sometimes do not meet completely.

Size	About 2.5 m.
Distribution	South-east Asia.
Habitat	Trees in forests and mangrove swamps. Nocturnal.
Food	Birds, lizards and small rodents.
Breeding	Egg-laying.
Notes	Distinctive, but sometimes confused with the Banded Krait (p.186), a dangerously venomous species. It is rear-fanged, the bite sometimes producing mild symptoms in humans. **POISONOUS**

BROWN TREE SNAKE *Boiga irregularis*

A slender tree snake with a wide head and large eyes. It is brown or reddish-brown with faint traces of darker crossbars, and has smooth scales. It is back-fanged, but not normally dangerous to humans.

Size	To 1.6 m.
Distribution	South-east Asia and the E seaboard of Australia.
Habitat	Trees, bushes and caves in tropical and subtropical forests. Often around human dwellings.
Food	Lizards, birds (including their eggs) and small mammals, especially bats.
Breeding	Egg-laying, with clutches of 4–10 eggs.
Notes	Accidentally introduced to the island of Guam in the late 1940s, it spread rapidly and caused the extinction of a number of songbird species.

SCARLET SNAKE *Cemophora coccinea*

A small burrowing snake with a cylindrical body, narrow, pointed head and smooth scales. It is brightly coloured with bands of red, white and black on the back, and the underside is plain white or cream.

Size	About 40 cm.
Distribution	SE USA.
Habitat	Loose, sandy soil. Also in rotting logs, under bark, etc.
Food	Snakes, lizards and nestling mice. Also eats snake eggs by chewing through the shell and forcing out the contents.
Breeding	Egg-laying.
Notes	The venomous Texas Coral Snake of the same region (p.193) has bands with red next to yellow. Kingsnakes and milksnakes (pp.126–132) have no white belly.

BANDED SAND SNAKE *Chilomeniscus cinctus*

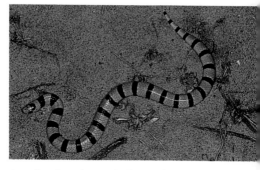

A small snake with smooth, shiny scales. Its head and snout are flattened and its lower jaw is inset. It is cream or yellow with black or dark brown crossbars down its back. The area between the bars is often reddish.

Size	To about 25 cm.
Distribution	The Sonoran Desert, in Arizona and NW Mexico.
Habitat	Sandy flats. It 'swims' through the sand and rarely comes to the surface.
Food	Sand-living insects, including centipedes and scorpions.
Breeding	Egg-laying, with clutches of 2–4 small eggs.
Notes	A second species, *C. stramineus*, is found in Baja California.

WESTERN SHOVEL-NOSED SNAKE *Chionactis occipitalis*

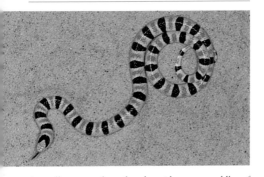

A small cream-coloured snake with narrow saddles of black, sometimes with red saddles between them. Its scales are smooth and shiny, the head is flattened from top to bottom and the snout is shaped like a shovel, for burrowing.

Size	To 40 cm.
Distribution	SW USA and adjacent parts of NW Mexico.
Habitat	Deserts. Along dry river beds, in dunes or loose sand. Appears on the surface at night.
Food	Insects and other invertebrates, including scorpions.
Breeding	Egg-laying, with clutches of about 4 eggs.
Notes	The Organ Pipe Shovel-nosed Snake, *C. palarostris*, has wider red bands and a smaller range, in S Arizona and Sonora, Mexico.

PARADISE TREE SNAKE *Chrysopelea paradisii*

A slender snake in which each scale is black with a yellow-green centre. Some have additional dark red markings along the back. Sometimes known as the 'flying snake' because it can parachute from high branches by spreading its ribs.

Size	To 1 m.
Distribution	South-east Asia.
Habitat	Forests and gardens, in trees and shrubs.
Food	Mainly lizards, also frogs and small rodents.
Breeding	Egg-laying.
Notes	There are other species of *Chrysopelea* in South-east Asia, but this is the commonest.

MUSSURANA *Clelia clelia*

A large snake with a cylindrical body, narrow head and smooth scales. The adult is completely black, but the young are red, with a black 'cap' on the top of their head and a white 'collar'. Rear-fanged, but harmless to humans.

Size	To 2.4 m.
Distribution	Central and South America.
Habitat	Forests.
Food	Other snakes, lizards and rodents.
Breeding	Egg-laying, with large clutches of up to 50 eggs.
Notes	There are 5 other species of *Clelia*, but these are rare and poorly known.

AMERICAN RACER *Coluber constrictor*

A slender, streamlined snake that is very fast-moving. It has smooth scales and occurs in a wide range of colours, including black, blue, grey, greenish, olive and brown. However, all the individuals in one area tend to be roughly the same colour. Its chin and throat are white.

Size	To 1.5 m.
Distribution	North and Central America, from Canada to Guatemala, except W USA.
Habitat	Open areas such as fields, edges of lakes and prairies. Active by day.
Food	Reptiles, birds and small mammals.
Breeding	Egg-laying, with clutches of 10–20 eggs or more.
Notes	Colour variation can make this snake difficult to identify.

85

BALKAN WHIPSNAKE *Coluber gemonensis*

A slender snake with smooth scales and large eyes. It is olive-brown with darker markings, especially on the front part of the body and in the young.

Size	To 1 m or slightly more.
Distribution	Greece, including some islands, and the E Adriatic coast.
Habitat	Open scrub, fields and waste ground. Active by day.
Food	Mainly lizards; also birds and small mammals.
Breeding	Egg-laying, with clutches of about 6–10 eggs.
Notes	There are several similar snakes in the region (pp.88 & 106). Look for the large eyes and quick movements.

HORSESHOE SNAKE *Coluber hippocrepis*

A slender snake with a bold pattern of large dark brown or black blotches running down the back. It has smaller dark spots on its sides, alternating with the large ones. Sometimes there is a horseshoe-shaped marking on the top of the head. The underside is orange or pink, especially when it is young.

Size	To 1.5 m.
Distribution	Portugal, S Spain, Sardinia and NW Africa.
Habitat	Dry, rocky places including stone walls. Active by day.
Food	Lizards, birds and rodents.
Breeding	Egg-laying.
Notes	The only large snake in its region with bold markings, and one of the few species to be active in the day.

LARGE WHIPSNAKE *Coluber jugularis*

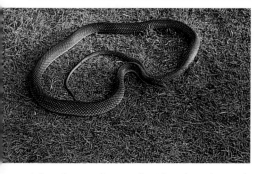

A long, brown, olive or yellowish snake with smooth scales and large eyes. There are faint lines running along the back of the adult, although these can be hard to make out. The young have short crossbars on their backs.

Size	To 2.5 m.
Distribution	SE Europe, including several islands, and parts of W Asia.
Habitat	Dry, open habitats including hillsides, fields, etc. Active by day.
Food	Lizards and small mammals.
Breeding	Egg-laying.
Notes	One of the largest European snakes and easily identified on this basis. The young are rather similar to several other species.

DAHL'S WHIPSNAKE *Coluber najadum dahli*

An extremely slender snake with a narrow head, large eyes and smooth scales. Its neck and the front part of its body are grey and the back half is brown or olive. It has a few large, round circles of black on the side of the neck.

Size	To about 1.3 m.
Distribution	SE Europe (Greece and the Balkan regions) and W Asia.
Habitat	Rocky hillsides and scrub. Also in fields and stone walls. Active by day.
Food	Lizards and small mammals.
Breeding	Egg-laying.
Notes	The most slender European snake.

Dark Green Whipsnake *Coluber viridiflavus*

A slender snake with large eyes. It is usually greenish or yellow with broad, irregular dark crossbars on the back and sides, changing to broken stripes on the tail. Some regions of Italy (including Sicily) have populations of completely black individuals.

Size	To 2 m, but usually less.
Distribution	Most of Central Europe, Italy and several Mediterranean islands.
Habitat	Dry, rocky places, lightly wooded areas and fields. Active by day.
Food	Lizards, small mammals and nestling birds.
Breeding	Egg-laying.
Notes	Darker than other day-active snakes in the region.

SMOOTH SNAKE *Coronella austriaca*

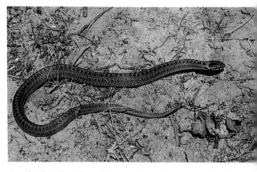

A cylindrical snake with smooth scales, a small head and small eyes. It is usually greyish with a series of small brown spots running down the back. The top of the head is dark and there are dark lines passing through its eyes.

Size	To 75 cm.
Distribution	Most of Europe, including S England, except most of Spain and Portugal. Also W Asia.
Habitat	Dry places such as heaths, open woods, railway embankments, etc. Active mostly by day, but secretive.
Food	Mostly lizards, but also small rodents. Constricts its prey.
Breeding	Live-bearing, with litters of about 10 young.
Notes	Britain's rarest reptile and protected there.

SOUTHERN SMOOTH SNAKE *Coronella girondica*

Similar to the Smooth Snake (p.91), but browner, more slender and with a more rounded snout. In regions where both species occur (e.g. Italy), the Smooth Snake is usually found at higher altitudes, where it is cooler.

Size	To about 60 cm.
Distribution	Spain, Portugal, SW France and Italy.
Habitat	Dry places, especially the edges of fields, stone walls, etc. Active mainly at night.
Food	Lizards.
Breeding	Egg-laying (in contrast to the Smooth Snake).
Notes	The Hooded Snake, *Macroprotodon cucullatus*, is similar, but has a bold black patch on the back of the neck.

AFRICAN EGG-EATING SNAKE *Dasypeltis scabra*

A slender snake with a cylindrical body and keeled scales. Its head is small and it has a very rounded snout. It is grey with two V-shaped marks on the head and a series of large dark blotches along the back. The inside of the mouth is black.

Size	To about 1 m, usually slightly less.
Distribution	Africa, S of the Sahara.
Habitat	Most places except deserts.
Food	Only birds' eggs: swallowed whole and crushed in the throat, then the empty shell is rejected.
Breeding	Egg-laying, with clutches of up to 25 eggs.
Notes	May be confused with several small vipers, which it mimics to avoid being attacked. It is, however, completely harmless.

EAST AFRICAN EGG-EATING SNAKE *Dasypeltis medici*

Similar in appearance to the common African Egg-Eating Snake (p.93), but more uniform in colour. It is light brown to buff with faint crossbars and flecks of white. The inside of the mouth is pink.

Size	To about 70 cm.
Distribution	E Africa.
Habitat	Forests.
Food	Only birds' eggs.
Breeding	Egg-laying.
Notes	Looks and behaves like a small viper. There are 6 species of egg-eaters altogether, but the 2 listed are among the most commonly seen, in the wild and in captivity.

PAINTED BRONZEBACK SNAKE *Dendrelaphis pictus*

A slender snake with a long tail. The body is brown or bronze and it has a white line, bordered with black, running along each flank. Another black line runs from the snout, through the eye and down to the angle of the jaw. When alarmed it flattens its neck from side to side.

Size	To 1 m.
Distribution	South-east Asia.
Habitat	Forests, fields and around villages. Active by day.
Food	Lizards and frogs.
Breeding	Egg-laying.
Notes	Distinguished from similar species by the black 'mask' together with the stripes down the sides.

RINGNECK SNAKE *Diadophis punctatus*

A dainty little snake with a slender body and small head. The body is light grey to black, but it nearly always has a bright yellow or orange band behind the head. Its belly is orange and its tail is red underneath. It may raise its tail to show off the bright coloration when it is frightened.

Size	30–75 cm, depending on subspecies.
Distribution	Throughout North America, but patchy in places.
Habitat	Damp places. Secretive, often under logs and rubbish.
Food	Worms, slugs, insects and small reptiles and amphibians.
Breeding	Egg-laying, with clutches of up to 10 eggs.
Notes	At least 10 subspecies, varying slightly in size and colour, and difficult to separate. Otherwise, cannot easily be confused with any other snake.

CATESBY'S SNAIL-EATING SNAKE *Dipsas catesbyi*

An extremely slender snake with smooth scales, a long tail, and a body that is flattened from side to side. Its head is broad, its snout rounded and its eyes are huge. It is black or dark brown with white circles along its back.

Size	To about 70 cm.
Distribution	The Amazon Basin, South America.
Habitat	Rain forests, where it is found in trees. Active by night.
Food	Slugs and snails. Specialised jaws help it to pull snails out of their shells.
Breeding	Egg-laying.
Notes	There are several similar species of *Dipsas*, but this is one of the more colourful and is quite common where it occurs.

☠ BOOMSLANG *Dispholidus typus*

A large, slender snake with a pointed head and large eyes. It varies greatly in colour: females are usually olive-brown and males are various shades of green or even blue with black edges to all their scales. When alarmed it puffs up its throat, displaying the brightly coloured skin between the scales.

Size	Usually to 1.5 m, sometimes slightly more.
Distribution	Most of Africa, except the Sahara.
Habitat	Grassland, scrub and lightly wooded areas. A good climber and active by day.
Food	Lizards (especially chameleons) and birds.
Breeding	Egg-laying, with clutches of 10–15 eggs.
Notes	One of the few back-fanged species that is **dangerous to humans**. Deaths have occurred. The large eyes are a good identification feature.

INDIGO SNAKE *Drymarchon corais couperi*

A large, glossy black snake with highly polished scales and an almost triangular body. Its chin may be dirty white or red. The young often have more red on their underside and bluish-white flecks on their sides.

Size	To 2 m, occasionally more.
Distribution	SE USA (mainly Florida).
Habitat	Sandy places, such as raised 'hammocks' in swamps. Active by day.
Food	Fish, amphibians, other reptiles, birds and small mammals.
Breeding	Egg-laying, with clutches of about 10 eggs.
Notes	Indigo snakes from other regions lack the glossy black coloration. Other North American black snakes (American Racer, p.85, and Black Pine Snake) have keeled scales.

BAIRD'S RATSNAKE *Elaphe bairdi*

A fairly slender snake with a long tail and flattened underside. Its head is narrow. The adult is grey or light brown, with four vague dusky lines running the length of the body. Each scale has an orange base, especially around the neck. Juveniles are grey with dark crossbars and lack the orange areas.

Size	To 1.5 m.
Distribution	S Texas and adjacent parts of Mexico.
Habitat	Rocky, wooded hillsides and canyons. Active mostly at night.
Food	Small mammals and birds.
Breeding	Egg-laying, with clutches of 5–15 eggs.
Notes	Adult is very distinctive, but juvenile could be confused with similar species.

TWIN-SPOTTED RATSNAKE *Elaphe bimaculata*

A moderately slender snake with a narrow head. Its ground colour is yellowish-brown or yellowish-grey and it has two types of markings. There may be two dark lines running the length of the snake (as shown above) or two parallel rows of small brown or reddish spots down the back.

Size	To about 75 cm.
Distribution	Central China.
Habitat	Hills and mountain foothills.
Food	Rodents.
Breeding	Egg-laying, with clutches of 6–12 eggs.
Notes	A similar species, *E. dione*, from China and further W, usually has less well-defined markings.

JAPANESE RATSNAKE *Elaphe climacophora*

A slender ratsnake with a long tail, which moves faster than many other ratsnakes. It is grey or olive and mottled with darker shades. It has a dark line from the eye to the angle of the jaw. In some forms the head is blue-grey and the body greenish.

Size	To 1.5 m.
Distribution	Japan.
Habitat	Fields and open spaces; sometimes in towns. Active by day or night.
Food	Rodents and birds.
Breeding	Egg-laying, with clutches of 6–10 eggs.
Notes	Colour may vary from island to island; otherwise, it is quite easy to identify. A naturally occurring albino population lives in and around the city of Iwakuni.

CENTRAL AMERICAN RATSNAKE *Elaphe flavirufa*

A very slender ratsnake with a long tail, broad head and large greyish-blue eyes. It is yellowish-brown with large blotches of reddish-brown along the back. Each blotch is bordered with black. The markings of young snakes are brighter than in the adult. The snake in the photograph is about to shed its skin.

Size	To 1.6 m.
Distribution	Central America, from Mexico to Nicaragua.
Habitat	Tropical forests. Active at night.
Food	Birds and small mammals.
Breeding	Egg-laying, with clutches of 4–10 eggs.
Notes	A very distinctive species, unlike any others in the region.

CORN SNAKE OR RED RATSNAKE *Elaphe guttata guttata*

A handsome ratsnake with large red saddles on a grey or yellowish background. Each saddle has a black border and there are smaller spots on the flanks. There is always a V-shaped mark on the top of the head. The underside is chequered in black and white.

Size	To 1.8 m, but usually less.
Distribution	E and SE USA.
Habitat	Wooded and rocky places. Often around human dwellings, in roofs, etc. Climbs well.
Food	Rodents and birds. The young also eat frogs.
Breeding	Egg-laying, with clutches of 10–20 eggs (exceptionally up to 40).
Notes	Easily identified by its coloration. A very popular pet and several mutations, such as albinos, are widely bred in captivity.

PLAINS RATSNAKE *Elaphe guttata emoryi*

Similar to the Corn Snake (opposite), but the saddles along its back are rich brown and it is stockier. There is some colour variation and the markings may appear 'washed out'.

Size	To 1.5 m.
Distribution	Central USA and NE Mexico.
Habitat	Canyons and hillsides, especially among rocks. Active at night during warm weather and by day at other times.
Food	Rodents and birds.
Breeding	Egg-laying, with clutches of up to 12 eggs. The eggs (and young) are larger than those of the Corn Snake.
Notes	Distinguished from other brown-blotched snakes in the region by a pointed mark between the eyes together with almost smooth scales.

105

AESCULAPIAN SNAKE *Elaphe longissima*

An elegant, slender snake with a narrow head. It is olive-brown with small flecks of white on the edges of some scales, especially in young snakes, which also have a pale yellowish spot on each side of the neck and a dark line through each eye.

Size	Usually about 1.5 m, but occasionally longer.
Distribution	Central and S Europe, except most of Spain and Portugal.
Habitat	Usually open woods and shrubby places. Also in overgrown fields and near stone walls, etc. Active by day or night.
Food	Birds and rodents, which are constricted.
Breeding	Egg-laying, with clutches of 6–12 eggs.
Notes	Similar to certain whipsnakes, but its scales are glossier and it does not move as quickly.

MANDARIN RATSNAKE *Elaphe mandarina*

A slender ratsnake with a long, narrow head. Its markings are especially striking: it has a row of yellow blotches running along the back, surrounded by black scales. The background colour is grey. Its head is marked with yellow and black chevrons.

Size	To about 1.5 m.
Distribution	S China and N Burma.
Habitat	Woods and fields in mountains, especially near water.
Food	Rodents and possibly birds.
Breeding	Egg-laying, with clutches of 4–10 eggs.
Notes	Not easily confused with other snakes.

GREY RATSNAKE *Elaphe obsoleta spiloides*

A form of the American ratsnake in which the adults and young are grey with irregular dark saddles (other subspecies lose their blotches as they grow). The scales on the back are weakly keeled, but those on the flanks are smooth.

Size	To over 2 m, but usually less.
Distribution	SE USA (Alabama, Mississippi, etc.)
Habitat	Wooded areas, hillsides, farms, etc. Climbs well. Active by day or night.
Food	Small mammals and birds.
Breeding	Egg-laying, with clutches of 20 or more eggs.
Notes	Texas Ratsnake, *E. o. lindheimeri*, may also be blotched, but is darker overall. Other ratsnakes lose their blotches as they grow.

EVERGLADES RATSNAKE *Elaphe obsoleta rossalleni*

A long and slender ratsnake with a bright orange or yellowish-orange background and four dusky lines along the body. The young are duller, and have grey blotches along their backs, which fade as the orange coloration develops at one to two years of age.

Size	To 2 m, but usually less.
Distribution	S Florida, USA.
Habitat	Open grassland, shrubs and pine trees. Climbs well. Active by day or night.
Food	Small mammals and birds. The young sometimes eat frogs.
Breeding	Egg-laying, with clutches of 6–20 eggs.
Notes	The Yellow Ratsnake, *E. o. quadrivittata*, is similar, but has a yellow or yellowish-brown background.

FOURLINED SNAKE *Elaphe quatuorlineata*

A bulky snake with a broad head and heavily keeled scales on the back. Greyish with four dark lines running down the back and sides and a dark line through each eye. Juveniles are grey with bold black blotches along their backs and some E European forms retain the blotches for life.

Size	Usually about 1.5 m, but may reach 2.5 m.
Distribution	Italy, SE Europe and SW Asia.
Habitat	Rocky hillsides, lightly wooded areas, humid valleys, etc. Sometimes near farms and villages.
Food	Small mammals, birds and their eggs.
Breeding	Egg-laying, with clutches of 6–20 eggs.
Notes	Adult is unlike other snakes from the region, but juvenile can be mistaken for European Cat Snake (p.168) or even some young vipers (pp.224–226).

LADDER SNAKE *Elaphe scalaris*

A moderately slender snake with a pointed snout and smooth scales. It is greyish-brown or brown, with a pair of dark stripes running down the back. Hatchlings are pale yellow or cream with dark crossbars, forming a 'ladder' pattern.

Size	To 1.5 m.
Distribution	Spain, Portugal, extreme SW France and Menorca.
Habitat	Rocky, scrubby hillsides, vineyards, olive groves, etc.
Food	Small mammals and birds, including eggs and nestlings.
Breeding	Egg-laying, with clutches of 6–12 eggs.
Notes	The Montpellier Snake (p.137) may be brown, but lacks the dark lines. Otherwise fairly distinctive. Young may be mistaken for vipers at first glance.

RUSSIAN RATSNAKE *Elaphe schrencki*

A slender ratsnake with a narrow head and slightly keeled scales on the back. It is black or dark brown, with narrow rings of yellow, white or greyish around the body. The scales around the lips are usually the same colour as the rings.

Size	To about 1.5 m.
Distribution	Central Asia, from S Siberia and China to Korea.
Habitat	Open forests, scrub, grasslands and farms. Active by day or night.
Food	Small mammals and birds.
Breeding	Egg-laying, with clutches of 6–12 eggs.
Notes	Not easily confused with other species, unless the light rings are missing or indistinct.

LEOPARD SNAKE *Elaphe situla*

A beautiful, dainty ratsnake with a slender body and narrow head. The background colour is cream or buff and the markings are brown, reddish-brown or dark red. Two forms sometimes occur together: one has a series of dark-edged blotches down the back and the other has a pair of stripes.

Size	To 1 m, but usually less.
Distribution	S Italy, Sicily, the Balkan region including many Adriatic islands, and Malta. Also parts of SW Asia.
Habitat	Rocky hillsides, dry stone walls, cultivated fields, etc. Active by day or night.
Food	Small rodents and birds.
Breeding	Egg-laying, with clutches of 2–7 elongated eggs.
Notes	Not easily confused with any other snake from the region.

Fox Snake *Elaphe vulpina*

A heavily built ratsnake with a bold pattern of dark chestnut-brown blotches down the back, on a grey or yellowish background. It has a row of smaller blotches on each flank. The head may be rust coloured, especially in the eastern subspecies, *gloydi*.

Size	To about 1.3 m.
Distribution	N-central USA and parts of S Canada.
Habitat	Prairies, woods, swamps and farmland.
Food	Small mammals.
Breeding	Egg-laying, with clutches of up to 10 eggs.
Notes	Several similar snakes in the region include the Eastern Hognose Snake (p.119), Bull Snake (p.154) and Copperhead (p.231). The Fox Snake rarely attempts to bite.

FISHING SNAKE *Erpeton tentaculatum*

A bizarre snake! Its body is almost rectangular in cross-section, it has heavily keeled scales and, most strangely, it has two fleshy 'tentacles' attached to the snout. These are thought to break up its outline. The markings are brown and cream lines running along the back.

Size	To about 60 cm.
Distribution	Thailand and S China.
Habitat	Completely aquatic; only in freshwater ponds and lakes.
Food	Fish, which are ambushed. The tentacles were previously thought to act as lures, but this idea has now been disproved.
Breeding	Live-bearing, with litters of up to 12 young.
Notes	Unmistakable – anyone can identify a fishing snake!

FALSE CORAL SNAKE *Erythrolamprus aesculapii*

A slender, cylindrical snake, with rings of red, black and white around the body. The red and black rings are always separated by narrow white ones. This and other 'false' coral snakes are thought to mimic the venomous coral snakes (pp.191–194), but this is by no means certain.

Size	To about 70 cm.
Distribution	Amazon Basin, from Trinidad to Ecuador, Bolivia and Brazil.
Habitat	Rain forests. Secretive; lives among leaf-litter, etc.
Food	Lizards, amphisbaenians and snakes.
Breeding	Unknown. Probably egg-laying.
Notes	There are many other black, red and white banded snakes in North, Central and South America, including several dangerous ones.

RED-TAILED RACER *Gonyosoma oxycephala*

A long, slender snake with a long tail and narrow, elegant head. Its head and body are bright green and the tail is rust-brown or orange. Each scale has a narrow black border, and it has a black line running from the snout, through the eye and onto the neck. It has a blue tongue.

Size	To 2 m.
Distribution	South-east Asia.
Habitat	Forests, where it lives mainly in trees and shrubs.
Food	Lizards, birds and small mammals.
Breeding	Egg-laying, with clutches of about 6 eggs.
Notes	Although there are other related green snakes, this is the most commonly seen species.

WESTERN HOGNOSE SNAKE *Heterodon nasicus*

A stocky little snake with a distinctive upturned snout. Its scales are heavily keeled, giving a rough appearance. Usually light brown or grey with blotches of brown, reddish-brown or olive along the back. It may pretend to be dead if it is disturbed.

Size	To about 70 cm.
Distribution	Central USA, also N into Canada and S into Mexico.
Habitat	Prairies, where it digs in dry, sandy soil.
Food	Amphibians, especially toads, and small rodents.
Breeding	Egg-laying, with clutches of 6–15 eggs.
Notes	Distinguished from other hognose snakes by extensive black areas on the underside.

EASTERN HOGNOSE SNAKE *Heterodon platyrhinos*

Similar to the Western Hognose Snake (opposite), but with several different colour patterns. Usually brown or tan with many indistinct blotches on the back and sides, but some specimens are plain black (above). It flattens its neck, hisses and may play dead if it is threatened.

Size	To 80 cm.
Distribution	Central, E and SE USA.
Habitat	Open places with sandy soil.
Food	Amphibians, especially toads.
Breeding	Egg-laying.
Notes	The only hognose snake with the underside of the tail paler than the belly.

SOUTHERN HOGNOSE SNAKE *Heterodon simus*

Smaller than the other hognose snakes, but with a similar body shape. The upturned snout is most pronounced in this species and it has a distinct ridge along the centre of the scale at the tip of the snout (the rostral scale). It is beige with rich brown blotches along the back.

Size	To 60 cm.
Distribution	SE USA (Florida and nearby states).
Habitat	Sandy fields and woods.
Food	Amphibians.
Breeding	Egg-laying.
Notes	Check the underside for positive identification: it is plain grey in this species.

SPOTTED NIGHT SNAKE *Hypsiglena torquata*

A small snake with smooth scales and a flattish head. Light brown or grey with a row of darker blotches along the back. There is usually a large dark area immediately behind the head, sometimes divided into two elongated blotches.

Size	To about 60 cm.
Distribution	S and SW USA and adjacent parts of Mexico.
Habitat	Very adaptable; moist and dry places, including desert, scrub, woods and meadows. Active only at night.
Food	Amphibians, small lizards and small mammals.
Breeding	Egg-laying, with clutches of 2–9 eggs.
Notes	Vertical pupils distinguish this snake from other similar species. Rear-fanged, but of no danger to man.

SLENDER VINE SNAKE *Imantodes cenchoa*

An almost unbelievably slender snake! Its body is pencil-thin, but the head is wide and looks swollen. It has large eyes with vertical pupils. It is pale brown with dark brown saddles along the back; sometimes these are broken in the middle to form two parallel rows of spots.

Size	To about 1 m, somtimes slightly more.
Distribution	Central and South America.
Habitat	Rain forests and tropical dry forests, where it lives entirely in trees and bushes.
Food	Tree frogs and small lizards.
Breeding	Egg-laying, with small clutches of elongated eggs.
Notes	There are 4 other species of *Imantodes* in Central and South America, but they are all very similar in appearance.

PRAIRIE KINGSNAKE *Lampropeltis calligaster*

A cylindrical snake with a small head and smooth scales. The markings vary; usually greyish with a row of brown or reddish-brown oval blotches along the back and other, less regular, blotches on the flanks. The markings may be indistinct, however, and some specimens are almost uniform brown.

Size	To 1 m.
Distribution	Central and SE USA, excluding most of Florida.
Habitat	Prairies, fields and forest clearings.
Food	Small reptiles, rodents and birds.
Breeding	Egg-laying, with clutches of 6–15 eggs.
Notes	The Mole Snake is a subspecies, *L. c. rhombomaculata*, with less blotches and less contrast between them and the background, which may be reddish-brown or olive.

CALIFORNIAN KINGSNAKE *Lampropeltis getulus californiae*

A rounded snake with smooth, shiny scales and a narrow head. It is black and white or brown and cream, but with variable markings. Usually banded, with narrow light bands alternating with wider dark ones, but sometimes with a light stripe along the back and another on each flank.

Size	To about 2 m, but usually much less.
Distribution	SW USA (mainly California and Arizona) and N Baja California, Mexico.
Habitat	Dry hillsides, scrubby and rocky places.
Food	Lizards, other snakes, birds and small mammals.
Breeding	Egg-laying, with clutches of 6–20 eggs.
Notes	Other banded kingsnakes include the Desert Kingsnake, *L. g. splendida*, which has much narrower light bands.

SPECKLED KINGSNAKE *Lampropeltis getulus holbrooki*

A cylindrical snake with smooth, shiny scales. It is black, with a white or yellow spot on each scale. Sometimes, the spots form a pattern of indistinct bands, with some more heavily spotted than others, especially where its range meets that of other subspecies.

Size	To 2 m.
Distribution	Central and S USA, essentially the Mississippi Basin.
Habitat	Very adaptable; moist and dry places, including swamps and lightly wooded areas.
Food	Amphibians, lizards, snakes, birds and small mammals.
Breeding	Egg-laying, with clutches of 6–20 eggs, or more.
Notes	The only kingsnake with a pattern of fairly even spots covering its body.

MEXICAN KINGSNAKE *Lampropeltis mexicana mexicana*

A fairly slender snake with smooth scales. The grey background has a number of narrow saddles along the back; each is dark red, bordered with black. The top of the head has a complex red figure, variable in shape.

Size	To about 75 cm.
Distribution	NE Mexico.
Habitat	Mountains, among rocks and scrub.
Food	Small mammals and birds.
Breeding	Egg-laying, with clutches of 4–10 eggs.
Notes	Other red-spotted snakes lack the distinctive head marking, which sometimes looks like a piece from a jigsaw puzzle.

GREY BANDED KINGSNAKE *Lampropeltis mexicana alterna*

A moderately slender snake with smooth scales. It has variable markings; wide red bands on a light grey or dark grey background, or narrow black bands on a light grey background are the commonest combinations. The bands usually have thin white edges.

Size To about 80 cm.

Distribution Chihuahuan Desert (extreme S Texas and adjacent parts of N Mexico).

Habitat Rocky canyons and hillsides, desert scrub.

Food Lizards, snakes and small mammals.

Breeding Egg-laying, with clutches of 4–10 eggs.

Notes Highly variable, with young of several forms sometimes hatching from a single clutch of eggs.

SONORAN MOUNTAIN KINGSNAKE *Lampropeltis pyromelana*

A slender kingsnake with smooth, glossy scales. It is red with black-bordered white rings around the body. The black edges are often wider towards the centre of the back and may meet, leaving wedges of red on each flank. The snout is always white, but it has a black area across the top of the head.

Size	To 1 m, usually somewhat less.
Distribution	SW Arizona and adjacent parts of N Mexico, with isolated populations in Utah and Nevada.
Habitat	Only in mountains, usually in lightly wooded and rocky places, often near streams. May be active by day.
Food	Lizards and small mammals.
Breeding	Egg-laying, with clutches of 3–8 eggs.
Notes	Distinguished from similar species by the white snout.

PUEBLAN MILKSNAKE *Lampropeltis triangulum campbelli*

A slender snake, although rather more thickset than some other milksnakes. The red, cream and black rings are fairly evenly spaced in this subspecies, except for the cream ring behind the head, which may be wider than the others.

Size	To 1 m.
Distribution	Central Mexico, mainly the state of Puebla.
Habitat	Rocky valleys.
Food	Reptiles and small mammals.
Breeding	Egg-laying, with clutches of 6–15 eggs.
Notes	One of the brightest milksnakes. Look for the evenly spaced body rings.

HONDURAN MILKSNAKE *Lampropeltis triangulum hondurensis*

A slender snake with smooth scales. It is red, with pairs of black rings around the body. The areas within these rings may be white, yellow or orange; sometimes they are the same shade as the rest of the body. Adults are usually darker than juveniles.

Size	To about 1.5 m, sometimes slightly more.
Distribution	E Honduras and Nicaragua, Central America.
Habitat	Tropical lowland forests.
Food	Lizards and small mammals.
Breeding	Egg-laying, with clutches of 5–10 eggs.
Notes	One of the largest milksnakes. The tips of the scales often become black in this subspecies.

SINALOAN MILKSNAKE *Lampropeltis triangulum sinaloae*

A slender snake with smooth scales. The predominant colour is red or orange, with widely spaced black–white–black rings. The head is black, with a white collar. Juveniles are often more brightly coloured than adults. It is nervous and quick moving, although it rarely bites.

Size	To about 1 m, usually less.
Distribution	Sinaloa State, Mexico and parts of nearby states.
Habitat	Dry lowland scrub and fields.
Food	Lizards and small mammals.
Breeding	Egg-laying, with clutches of 3–8 eggs.
Notes	Distinguished from most other milksnakes by the wide red areas between the black and white rings.

CALIFORNIAN MOUNTAIN KINGSNAKE *Lampropeltis zonata*

A slender snake with smooth scales and a cylindrical body. It is bright red, with narrow rings of white, bordered with black. The black areas are often wider along the middle of the back and may touch, especially towards the tail, reducing the amount of red present. The snout is black.

Size	To 1 m, usually less.
Distribution	California and S Washington, USA, and Baja California, Mexico.
Habitat	Mountains. Among rockpiles, especially in coniferous forests.
Food	Lizards, snakes, birds and small mammals.
Breeding	Egg-laying, with clutches of 3–8 eggs.
Notes	The narrow rings and the black snout should distinguish it from similar species.

AURORA HOUSE SNAKE *Lamprophis aurora*

A stocky snake with smooth, shiny scales and a narrow head. The adult is olive-green with a thin orange line running along the centre of the back. Juveniles are more brightly coloured with specks of lime-green on each scale, and the orange line is more prominent.

Size	To about 60 cm.
Distribution	SE South Africa.
Habitat	Grassland and scrub.
Food	Small rodents. The young also eat small lizards.
Breeding	Egg-laying, with clutches of 8–12 eggs.
Notes	Its coloration makes this snake unmistakable.

Brown House Snake *Lamprophis fuliginosus*

Medium-built with small, smooth scales and large eyes. It is uniform brown, reddish-brown, orange or almost black, except for a cream line that runs from the top of the snout, over each eye and onto the neck. The underside is pinkish-white and highly glossy.

Size	To about 1 m, sometimes slightly more.
Distribution	S half of Africa.
Habitat	Grassland, scrub and farmland. Often around villages, farms and even in large towns and cities.
Food	Mostly rodents, also other small mammals and lizards. A powerful constrictor.
Breeding	Egg-laying, with clutches of 8–15 eggs. May lay several clutches of eggs each year.
Notes	Certain other house snakes are similar, but rare. The pale streaks over the eyes are fairly distinctive.

CAT-EYED SNAKE *Leptodeira septentrionalis*

A slender snake with smooth scales, a broad head and large eyes, which have vertical pupils. Its body is cream or light brown and there is a series of irregular dark brown or black blotches along the back.

Size	To about 1 m.
Distribution	From S Texas (just), through Central America and into N South America.
Habitat	Humid places, near streams and ponds or in moist forests. Active only at night.
Food	Frogs, including the eggs of species that breed in bushes overhanging water.
Breeding	Egg-laying.
Notes	A common tropical and subtropical species that may cause identification problems. Rear-fanged, but not dangerous to humans.

PARROT SNAKE *Leptophis ahaetulla*

A slender snake with a long, narrow head and keeled scales. Usually bright green, but variable. There may be a black line passing through the eye, but this is sometimes missing. Also, the flanks may be marked with yellow or brown. It opens its mouth widely when threatened.

Size	To 2 m.
Distribution	Tropical Central America and much of South America.
Habitat	Wet or dry forests. Usually in trees or shrubs.
Food	Lizards, birds and small mammals.
Breeding	Egg-laying.
Notes	There are 6 other species, all similar in appearance, but this is the most widespread and common.

MONTPELLIER SNAKE *Malpolon monspessulanus*

A muscular snake with smooth scales and distinctive large eyes, over which is a ridged scale giving the snake a fierce expression. Uniform in colour, but variable: brown, rust, grey, olive or even black. Very fast-moving and aggressive.

Size	To 2 m; among the largest European snakes.
Distribution	Spain, Portugal, S France, Balkan region, N Africa and SW Asia.
Habitat	Dry, open places. Mediterranean scrub (maquis), vineyards, hillsides, marshes, etc.
Food	Lizards, snakes, nestling birds, small mammals.
Breeding	Egg-laying.
Notes	Usually identified by its large size, uniform colour and speed. Rear-fanged, producing swelling and other symptoms in humans.

SONORAN WHIPSNAKE *Masticophis bilineatus*

A long, slender snake with a streamlined head and large eyes. Its body is grey or olive above with one thin and one thick line along each flank. A black line passes from the snout to the angle of the jaw, just below each eye; the lip scales below this line are white.

Size	To about 1.6 m.
Distribution	Sonoran Desert (SE Arizona and adjacent parts of NE Mexico.
Habitat	Dry mountain foothills, often among sparse trees, shrubs and large cacti.
Food	Birds, lizards and frogs. An active daytime hunter.
Breeding	Egg-laying, with clutches of 6–13 eggs.
Notes	Other whipsnakes lack the white lines on the flanks and the bold black line along the side of the head.

COACHWHIP SNAKE *Masticophis flagellum*

A slender snake with a long tail, smooth scales and large eyes. Usually quite uniform brown, tan, grey or pinkish, or with indistinct bands, especially on the front of the body. The shape of the scales on the tail is very suggestive of a plaited whip.

Size	To 2.5 m.
Distribution	S USA from California to Florida and adjacent parts of N Mexico. There are many subspecies.
Habitat	Highly varied, from deserts to woods and farmland.
Food	Lizards, snakes, birds and their eggs, small mammals.
Breeding	Egg-laying, with clutches of up to 20 eggs.
Notes	Whipsnakes, coachwhips and racers can be hard to identify; fast-moving snakes with uniform colour (not black) are normally this species.

VIPERINE SNAKE *Natrix maura*

The adult is quite stocky, juveniles more slender. The scales are heavily keeled and the eyes are set towards the top of the head. It is olive, brown, greenish or reddish with two rows of dark blotches along the back, sometimes forming a zigzag. Occasionally there is a pair of light yellow stripes down the back.

Size	To about 75 cm, usually less.
Distribution	Spain, Portugal, SW France and N Africa.
Habitat	Near water: around ponds, slow-moving rivers and marshes, including salt marshes.
Food	Frogs, toads and tadpoles, fish and earthworms.
Breeding	Egg-laying.
Notes	The Grass Snake (opposite) usually has a bold white or yellow collar and the Dice Snake (p.142) is less distinctly marked.

GRASS SNAKE *Natrix natrix*

A slender snake with keeled scales. It is usually olive-brown, with a row of short black bars or spots on each flank. Sometimes (from Italy and SE Europe) it has a pair of pale yellow stripes along the length of the body, and it normally has a pair of yellow or cream patches behind the head; these may join to form a complete ring or collar. The snake pictured above is feigning death.

Size	To 1.5 m, occasionally more.
Distribution	SW Asia, NW Africa and most of Europe.
Habitat	Damp meadows, alongside streams and canals, and in lightly wooded areas.
Food	Amphibians and fish.
Breeding	Egg-laying, with clutches of 20 or more eggs, laid in rotting leaves, compost or manure heaps.
Notes	The yellow collar separates it from similar snakes.

DICE SNAKE *Natrix tessellata*

A stocky snake with a narrow head and strongly keeled scales, giving a rough appearance. Usually brown, grey or greenish, with indistinct spots scattered all over the back and sides, sometimes joined to form short bars. Its eyes and nostrils point upwards.

Size	Females to 1 m, males to about 75 cm.
Distribution	Italy, SE Europe, SW and central Asia.
Habitat	More aquatic than the Grass Snake (p.141), often seen in water.
Food	Fish and amphibians.
Breeding	Egg-laying.
Notes	Its range distingushes it from the Viperine Snake (p.140); the Grass Snake (p.141) is larger, with a light collar marking.

GREEN WATER SNAKE *Nerodia cyclopion*

A stocky snake with strongly keeled scales, a triangular head and small eyes pointed slightly upwards. It is greenish-brown overall, sometimes with indistinct mottling of a slightly darker shade.

Size	To about 1.3 m.
Distribution	Florida and parts of nearby states (subspecies *floridana*), and the Mississippi Basin (subspecies *cyclopion*).
Habitat	Swamps, margins of lakes, ponds, etc.
Food	Fish and amphibians.
Breeding	Live-bearing, with litters of up to 50 young.
Notes	American water snakes can be hard to tell apart or from the venomous Cottonmouth (p.232). They should not be handled unless identification is certain.

BANDED WATER SNAKE *Nerodia fasciata*

A stout snake with a wide head and strongly keeled scales. Usually banded, but the width of the bands, and the colour, is highly variable. It may be brown, tan, yellow, orange or red in almost any combination. A dark line joins the eye with the angle of the jaw. The subspecies *compressicanda* (pictured above) has a flattened tail and its bands may be indistinct.

Size	To about 1 m.
Distribution	SE USA.
Habitat	Streams, ponds, lakes and swamps.
Food	Fish and amphibians.
Breeding	Live-bearing, with litters of 10–20 young.
Notes	The dark line on the side of the face is a fairly reliable identification guide, but see the notes for the Green Water Snake (p.143).

NORTHERN WATER SNAKE *Nerodia sipedon*

A heavy-bodied snake with keeled scales and a variable pattern of bands. It can be almost any shade from light grey to dark brown, with markings of red to black. Large specimens may seem almost uniform in colour, especially when out of the water.

Size	To about 1 m.
Distribution	E and central USA, except the extreme SE.
Habitat	Swamps, marshes, ponds and streams. Very common.
Food	Fish and amphibians.
Breeding	Live-bearing, with large litters of young.
Notes	Can be difficult to identify with certainty. The Banded Water Snake (opposite) has a line through the eye and its range does not overlap with this species or its subspecies.

Brown Water Snake *Nerodia taxispilota*

A heavy-bodied snake with a broad head, keeled scales and a variable pattern of dark brown blotches on a lighter background. Large specimens may seem almost uniform brown, especially out of the water.

Size	To about 1.5 m.
Distribution	SE USA, including all Florida and parts of adjacent states.
Habitat	Swamps, marshes, ponds and streams. Very common in places.
Food	Fish and amphibians.
Breeding	Live-bearing, with large litters of young.
Notes	Can be difficult to identify with certainty. Often mistaken for the venomous Cottonmouth (p.232), which is usually darker in colour.

ROUGH GREEN SNAKE *Opheodryas aestivus*

A slender snake with a graceful, narrow head. Its scales are keeled. Usually bright grass-green, with a paler, sometimes white, underside. It has large eyes with round pupils.

Size	To about 85 cm.
Distribution	E USA and NE Mexico.
Habitat	Heavily overgrown areas, along streams and rivers, among shrubs, etc. A good climber.
Food	Insects and spiders.
Breeding	Egg-laying, with clutches of 3–6 eggs.
Notes	Very distinctive. Smooth Green Snake (p.148) has smooth scales.

Smooth Green Snake *Opheodryas vernalis*

A very slender snake with smooth scales. It is bright green above and white below, although the young may be brown or olive. Very dainty in appearance.

Size To about 50 cm.

Distribution NE and parts of central North America.

Habitat Grasslands, fields and lightly wooded areas. It rarely climbs.

Food Insects and spiders.

Breeding Normally egg-laying, although eggs sometimes hatch within a few days of laying. It is even possible that it gives birth to live young in northern parts of its range.

Notes The Rough Green Snake (p.147) has keeled scales.

VINE SNAKE *Oxybelis aeneus*

An extremely slender snake with an elongated head and sharply pointed snout. It is brown or grey, and paler towards the head. The top of the head is darker than the lips and chin and there is a dark line through the eye.

Size	To 1.5 m.
Distribution	From extreme S Arizona, through Mexico and Central America, into South America.
Habitat	Trees and shrubs in dry or moist scrub or forests.
Food	Lizards.
Breeding	Egg-laying, with clutches of 3–5 eggs.
Notes	There are other vine snakes in parts of Central and South America, many being very similar to one another. Rear-fanged, but of no threat to humans.

SPOTTED GREEN SNAKE *Philothamnus semivariegatus*

A very slender snake with strongly keeled scales. Its head is flattened and bluish and its eyes are large with round pupils. The rest of the body is bright green with darker spots on the front half, sometimes arranged into short bars. It has a long tail.

Size	To about 1 m.
Distribution	Most of Africa, except the Sahara and other dry regions.
Habitat	Bushes, trees and dense vegetation, usually near rocks or watercourses.
Food	Lizards, including chameleons, and frogs.
Breeding	Egg-laying, with clutches of 3–12 eggs.
Notes	Several other species of *Philothamnus* look rather similar, but this is the most widespread.

SADDLED LEAF-NOSED SNAKE *Phyllorhynchus browni*

A short, well-built snake with an enlarged, leaf-shaped scale that curls up onto the top of the snout and is used in burrowing. Its body scales are smooth and it is buff or cream with large blotches or saddles of darker brown.

Size	To about 50 cm.
Distribution	S Arizona and NW Mexico.
Habitat	Desert scrub.
Food	Probably lizards, especially geckos, and their eggs.
Breeding	Egg-laying, with clutches of 2–5 eggs.
Notes	The enlarged rostral scale and bold markings are distinctive. Poorly known and rarely seen, except on desert roads at night.

Sonoran Gopher Snake *Pituophis melanoleucus affinis*

A moderately slender snake with heavily keeled scales. Its eyes are large with round pupils. Its background colour is yellowish or cream and the blotches along its back are rust coloured. It is more placid than the Bull Snake (p.154) and rarely bites.

Size	To about 2 m.
Distribution	Arizona, parts of New Mexico, and NW Mexico.
Habitat	Deserts and desert scrublands.
Food	Small mammals and birds.
Breeding	Egg-laying, with clutches of 2–15 eggs.
Notes	Other gopher snakes are similar, but the Sonoran subspecies tends to be a rustier colour and better natured.

NORTHERN PINE SNAKE *Pituophis melanoleucus melanoleucus*

A large snake with keeled scales and a pointed snout. It has a white, cream or pale yellow background, with a series of large black or dark brown blotches along the back. A bad-tempered subspecies that often hisses loudly and strikes vigorously.

Size	To nearly 2 m.
Distribution	Parts of E USA in suitable habitat.
Habitat	Sandy places, often associated with pinewoods. A good burrower. Active by day and night.
Food	Small mammals and birds.
Breeding	Egg-laying, with clutches of 5–10 eggs.
Notes	The Southern Pine Snake, *P. m. mugitus*, has less well-defined blotches and the Black Pine Snake, *P. m. lodingi*, is completely black.

BULL SNAKE *Pituophis melanoleucus sayi*

A large and powerful snake with very heavily keeled scales. It has a pointed snout, and a dark line runs across the top of the head, through each eye and on to the angles of the jaw. Its body is yellowish-brown with large brown or rust-coloured blotches. A fierce snake that hisses loudly if upset, and it may bite.

Size	To 2.5 m.
Distribution	Central North America from the Canadian border to Mexico.
Habitat	Very adaptable. In deserts, prairies and farmland.
Food	Small mammals and birds.
Breeding	Egg-laying, with clutches of up to 24 eggs.
Notes	This is the largest form of a variable species. Other subspecies are described on the previous pages.

NAMIB SAND SNAKE *Psammophis leightoni*

An extremely elongated and slender snake with smooth scales and a pointed head, distinct from the body. Its eyes are large and have a dark line passing through them. Otherwise, it is light brown to beige, with a broad, darker line running along the back.

Size	To about 1 m.
Distribution	S Africa.
Habitat	Desert, semi-desert regions and scrub. Active by day.
Food	Mainly lizards, but also rodents and other snakes.
Breeding	Egg-laying, with clutches of about 6 eggs.
Notes	There are several other similar species of *Psammophis*. Rear-fanged, but not dangerous to humans.

HISSING SAND SNAKE *Psammophis sibilans*

A slender snake with a long tail, smooth scales and large eyes. There are several forms, but most are mainly light brown to olive, with light and dark stripes on the flanks. It may have pale bars on the neck.

Size	To just over 1 m.
Distribution	Throughout Africa, in suitable habitat.
Habitat	Grasslands and dry, rocky places. Alert and fast-moving; hunts by day.
Food	Mainly lizards, also birds and small mammals.
Breeding	Egg-laying, with clutches of 4–15 eggs.
Notes	There are several similar sand snakes, but this is the most widely distributed and one of the largest. Rear-fanged and capable of a painful, though not dangerous, bite to humans.

MOLE SNAKE *Pseudaspis cana*

A large, thick-bodied snake whose head is no wider than its body. Its snout is slightly 'hooked'. It usually has smooth scales, but the colour is highly variable: adults may be plain black, brown or reddish, but sometimes they are blotched. Juveniles are always blotched.

Size	To 2 m, usually slightly less.
Distribution	S and E Africa.
Habitat	Grassland, scrub and semi-desert from sea level to mountains.
Food	Mammals, including rodents. Often tolerated around houses and farms because they control vermin.
Breeding	Live-bearing, with litters of 25–40, although litters of almost 100 have been recorded.
Notes	Adults are quite distinctive due to their size.

157

ASIATIC RATSNAKE *Ptyas korros*

A large, powerful constricting snake with keeled scales. It is uniform greyish-brown, paler below, and has large dark eyes. It is often killed in large numbers for the skin trade.

Size	To 2.2 m.
Distribution	South-east Asia.
Habitat	Forests, fields and around villages.
Food	Small mammals.
Breeding	Egg-laying.
Notes	There are several other large ratsnakes in the region, but the plain colour and large eyes help to identify this species.

LONG-NOSED SNAKE *Rhinocheilus lecontei*

A slender snake with a cylindrical body and smooth scales. It has a pointed head and the snout overhangs the lower jaw. It is cream or yellowish with a row of white-edged, black saddles down the back. The spaces between the saddles have flecks of black and patches of red scales.

Size	To about 1 m, usually rather less.
Distribution	S USA and N Mexico.
Habitat	Deserts, scrub and dry grasslands. Usually active in the evening or night.
Food	Mainly lizards, also snakes, birds and mammals.
Breeding	Egg-laying, with clutches of 4–11 eggs.
Notes	Similar to milksnakes (pp.129–131), mountain kingsnakes (pp.124 & 128) and coral snakes (pp.191–194), but black markings are saddles.

WESTERN PATCH-NOSED SNAKE *Salvadora hexalepis*

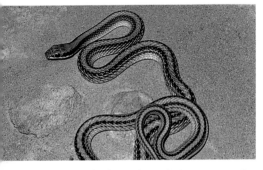

An active, slender snake with large eyes and a distinctive, upturned scale at the tip of the snout. It is beige or cream with two pairs of darker lines running along the back, either side of a lighter central area. The underside is white or cream.

Size	To about 1 m.
Distribution	SW USA and NW Mexico.
Habitat	Dry places, especially dry grasslands and desert scrub. Fast-moving and active by day.
Food	Lizards and their eggs, small mammals.
Breeding	Egg-laying, with clutches of 4–10 eggs.
Notes	Graham's Patch-nosed Snake, *S. grahamiae*, has only a single dark line each side of the central, lighter one.

CENTIPEDE SNAKE *Scolecophis atrocinctus*

A slender snake with smooth scales, a small head and small eyes. Its coloration is very distinctive: it has black and white rings around the body and tail, with brilliant red markings along the top of every white band. It has a prominent white band over its snout.

Size	To about 70 cm.
Distribution	Central America, from Guatamala to Costa Rica.
Habitat	Lowland dry and moist forests.
Food	Centipedes and possibly other invertebrates.
Breeding	Unknown, but probably egg-laying.
Notes	An interesting but very poorly known snake.

ROSALIA RATSNAKE *Senticolis rosaliae*

A snake of medium build with a long, narrow head and smooth scales. It is olive, brown or reddish-brown with no markings, although juveniles have light-coloured bars across the back and light markings on the head and neck.

Size	To 1.5 m.
Distribution	Baja California, Mexico.
Habitat	Humid canyons in mountain ranges. Active mainly at night.
Food	Small mammals.
Breeding	Egg-laying, with clutches of 3–8 eggs.
Notes	The only plain brown snake from the area. Other ratsnakes, *Elaphe* and *Bogertophis*, all have some markings.

CLOUDED SLUG-EATING SNAKE *Sibon nebulata*

An extremely slender snake with a wide head that is
very distinct from its body, which is slightly flattened
from side to side. It has large eyes and smooth scales,
and is brownish, with mottled lighter markings.

Size	To about 80 cm.
Distribution	Central and N South America.
Habitat	Rain forests, where it lives in trees, orchids, airplants etc.
Food	Slugs and snails. Its jaws are specially adapted to extract the soft parts of snails from their shells.
Breeding	Egg-laying.
Notes	There are several species of *Sibon* and related species in Central and South America, of which this is the most widespread.

SOUTH AMERICAN TIGER SNAKE *Spilotes pullatus*

A long, slender snake with large, keeled scales. The body is flattened from side to side and the head is very distinct from the neck. Its eyes are large and prominent. Variable in colour, but usually yellowish with black bars or streaks; sometimes black, with yellow bars and spots.

Size	To about 2.5 m.
Distribution	Central America and much of South America.
Habitat	Wet or dry tropical forests, where it is usually in trees or shrubs.
Food	Birds and small mammals.
Breeding	Egg-laying.
Notes	An unmistakable species. Often aggressive.

DeKay's Snake *Storeria dekayi*

A tiny snake with keeled scales and a narrow head that is not much wider than its body. It is light to dark brown with two rows of dark spots running down the back. It has a short dark streak down the side of the head.

Size	To about 35 cm.
Distribution	The entire E half of the USA and NE Mexico.
Habitat	Damp places in fields, woods, swamps, gardens and parks.
Food	Earthworms and possibly other invertebrates.
Breeding	Live-bearing, usually with litters of about 4–6 tiny young, but sometimes 3–27.
Notes	Can be confused with the young of other brown-coloured snakes: look for the paired dark spots running down the back.

RED-BELLIED SNAKE *Storeria occiptomaculata*

Quite a stout little snake with keeled scales and a small head. It is brown or grey with, sometimes, four faint dark lines along the back. It has three pale-coloured blotches just behind the head and the underside is bright red to yellowish-orange.

Size	To about 30 cm.
Distribution	E half of North America, from S Canada to Florida and the Gulf coast.
Habitat	Very secretive; usually under logs, stones and rubbish in damp places.
Food	Earthworms and other soft-bodied invertebrates.
Breeding	Live-bearing, with litters of 6 or more small young.
Notes	The only small snake with a dark upperside, a plain red or orange belly, but no light-coloured collar (see Ringneck Snake, p.96).

BLACK-HEADED SNAKE *Tantilla nigriceps*

A small and slender snake with smooth scales. It is yellowish-brown with a white underside and a black 'cap' on the head, extending onto the neck.

Size	To about 30 cm, but often smaller.
Distribution	The Great Plains of North America and nearby parts of Mexico.
Habitat	Dry sandy places, usually under rocks, logs, etc. May be seen crossing roads at night.
Food	Centipedes, insect larvae, etc.
Breeding	Egg-laying, with clutches of 1–3 eggs.
Notes	There are about 50 species of black-headed snakes, found from North America to Argentina, which all look very similar. They may be identified by location, otherwise an expert opinion is needed.

EUROPEAN CAT SNAKE *Telescopus fallax*

A slender snake with smooth scales, a broad head and blunt snout. Its small eyes have vertical pupils. It is usually grey or brownish, with a dark blotch just behind the head and more dark spots along the back and sides.

Size	To about 75 cm, occasionally larger.
Distribution	SE Europe, including many islands, and SW Asia.
Habitat	Rocky places, especially in mountains, among stone walls, etc. Active only at night.
Food	Lizards, which are caught at night while asleep.
Breeding	Egg-laying.
Notes	The only slender snake in the area with vertical pupils. Sometimes mistaken for vipers, which are thicker and have keeled scales. Rear-fanged, but harmless to humans.

AFRICAN TIGER SNAKE *Telescopus semiannulatus*

A slender snake with smooth scales, a broad head and large eyes. Its eyes have vertical pupils. It has an orange head and the rest of the body may also be orange, but is sometimes pinkish, brownish or mustard yellow. It has a row of widely spaced, dark blotches along the back.

Size	To about 1 m.
Distribution	E and S Africa.
Habitat	Semi-arid savannah.
Food	Lizards, small rodents and birds.
Breeding	Egg-laying, with clutches of 6–20 eggs.
Notes	A similar species, the Namib Tiger Snake, *T. beetzi*, is found in parts of its range, but it is paler and also rare.

BLACK-NECKED GARTER SNAKE *Thamnophis cyrtopsis*

A slender snake with strongly keeled scales, a narrow head and large eyes. It has a large black spot behind the head, which is bisected by an orange line that runs right along the back. It also has a yellowish stripe on each flank and dark blotches between the stripes.

Size	To about 75 cm.
Distribution	S-central USA, extending into Mexico.
Habitat	Near water in an otherwise arid region. Active by day.
Food	Amphibians (frogs and tadpoles).
Breeding	Live-bearing, with litters of about 6 young (rarely up to 20). The young are larger than those of other garter snakes.
Notes	The bright orange dorsal stripe, combined with the black markings on the neck, distinguish it from other garter snakes.

TERRESTRIAL GARTER SNAKE *Thamnophis elegans*

Quite a large, chunky garter snake, with keeled scales. Its markings are highly variable, but it usually has a prominent stripe down the back and another on each flank. The area between the stripes is pale and spotted, or dark and flecked with white.

Size	To about 1 m.
Distribution	Most of the W half of the USA, excluding deserts, and adjacent parts of SW Canada.
Habitat	Grasslands and lightly wooded areas, usually in damp places, but sometimes in fields. Often less aquatic than other garter snakes.
Food	Amphibians and rodents.
Breeding	Live-bearing, with litters of 4–15 young.
Notes	There are several similar species of garter snake. Look for the bold dorsal stripe.

CHEQUERED GARTER SNAKE *Thamnophis marcianus*

A thick-bodied garter snake with a broad head. It has a buff, yellowish-brown or greenish-yellow background with a chequered pattern of large, square-shaped black blotches down the back, divided by a narrow cream or yellow stripe.

Size	To about 1 m, but usually smaller.
Distribution	Texas and neighbouring states, parts of Arizona and SE California, and adjacent parts of Mexico.
Habitat	Near rivers, streams and irrigation ditches in arid and grassland areas.
Food	Fish, frogs, tadpoles, lizards and small rodents.
Breeding	Live-bearing, with litters of 6–18 young.
Notes	A distinctive garter snake: look for the chequered pattern along the back.

WESTERN RIBBON SNAKE *Thamnophis proximus*

A slender snake with a narrow head and keeled scales. It has an orange stripe down the centre of the back and a cream or pale yellow stripe on each flank; the area between is usually brown or olive. The scales around the mouth are very light coloured compared with the top of the head.

Size	To about 1.2 m.
Distribution	The Gulf coast of the USA, N along the Mississippi valley and S into Mexico and Central America.
Habitat	Varied; in and around woodlands, marshes, lakesides and tropical forests.
Food	Frogs, tadpoles, fish, insects and earthworms.
Breeding	Live-bearing, with litters of 4–27 young.
Notes	The orange stripe distinguishes it from other ribbon snakes (see p.175). Garter snakes are stouter.

173

PLAINS GARTER SNAKE *Thamnophis radix*

A slender snake with keeled scales and a narrow head. It has a bright orange stripe down the centre of the back and a yellow or cream stripe on each flank. Between the stripes it is olive, with small dark spots or, sometimes, almost uniformly dark. There are black bars on the otherwise yellow scales around the mouth.

Size	To about 85 cm.
Distribution	N-central USA and adjacent parts of Canada.
Habitat	Prairies and farmland, near water.
Food	Amphibians, fish and earthworms.
Breeding	Live-bearing, with litters of up to 50 young.
Notes	The bright orange stripe and dark markings on the lips will usually distinguish it from other garter snakes.

EASTERN RIBBON SNAKE *Thamnophis sauritus*

A slender snake, with keeled scales and a narrow head. It has a yellow stripe down the centre of the back and another on each flank, usually of the same colour. It has a double row of black spots between the stripes, but these may not be visible unless the skin is stretched.

Size	To about 75 cm, occasionally longer.
Distribution	The entire E half of the USA, from New England to Florida and W to Louisiana.
Habitat	Marshes and the edges of rivers, ponds and lakes.
Food	Amphibians and fish.
Breeding	Live-bearing, with litters of up to 16 young.
Notes	The only ribbon snake with three stripes of the same colour. Garter snakes have thicker bodies.

EASTERN GARTER SNAKE *Thamnophis sirtalis*

A slender snake with keeled scales. This species is highly variable. It has three pale stripes, the one on the back being the brightest, and may have red markings between the stripes. Otherwise mainly olive, grey, bluish or brown.

Size	To 1 m or slightly more.
Distribution	Most of the USA, except the SW, and S Canada.
Habitat	Varied; grassland, farmland, city parks, etc., invariably near water.
Food	Amphibians, fish, small mammals and birds, and earthworms.
Breeding	Live-bearing, with clutches of up to 100 young, but more usually 10–20.
Notes	Easily confused with other garter snakes, but often the most common species in its region.

TWIG SNAKE *Thelotornis kirtlandii*

A extremely slender, elongated snake, with a long tail, narrow head and pointed snout. Its eyes have horizontal pupils, shaped like keyholes, which helps it to judge distances. It is greyish-brown with faint light and dark markings. It inflates its neck when annoyed, to display bold black markings between the scales.

Size	To about 1 m, occasionally longer.
Distribution	Central and W Africa.
Habitat	Rain forests.
Food	Lizards and small birds.
Breeding	Egg-laying, with clutches of 4–18 elongated eggs.
Notes	A second species of Twig Snake, *T. capensis*, from S and E Africa, is similar in appearance.

LYRE SNAKE *Trimorphodon biscutatus*

A slender snake with a long tail, smooth scales and a broad, flattened head. Its large eyes have vertical pupils. It is light brown or grey, with large brown blotches along the back, each blotch having a paler centre. It is supposed to have a lyre-shaped marking on the head, but this can be difficult to make out.

Size	To about 1 m, occasionally slightly longer.
Distribution	Arid regions of SW USA and adjacent parts of Mexico.
Habitat	Dry, rocky places. Active only at night.
Food	Lizards, birds and small mammals, including bats.
Breeding	Egg-laying, with clutches of 6–20 eggs.
Notes	The combination of large blotches and vertical pupils distinguish it from other North American snakes. Rear-fanged, but not thought to be dangerous to humans.

BURROWING ASPS (ATRACTASPIDIAE)

The burrowing asps are a small group of snakes whose relationships with other snakes are uncertain. There are about sixty species altogether, and they are mostly confined to Africa, although one species occurs in the Middle East.

Their heads are small and have large plate-like scales covering them. Their eyes are very small. Their bodies are smooth and shiny and their tails are short. Burrowing asps only appear on the surface at night, spending most of their time in underground burrows or hidden in leaf-litter or sandy soil. They prey on other burrowing animals including rodents, lizards, worm lizards and other snakes. Some species are highly specialised and only eat certain species of invertebrates.

Members of the genus *Atractaspis* have large hollow fangs but no other teeth. The fangs can be folded and some species are able to erect them without fully opening their mouth, so that they project out of the side. This is thought to help them to bite their prey while they are in the confines of a burrow. They bite with a sideways stab and are difficult to handle safely. They have large venom glands but their venom is not very toxic to humans – bites usually result in localised swellings and pain although some species have caused fatalities. Other species have fixed front fangs or fangs at the back of their mouths.

In the past, burrowing asps have been classified with the vipers, and were called 'mole vipers'. Now they are thought to be most closely related to the harmless and back-fanged snakes, Colubridae.

CAPE CENTIPEDE-EATER *Aparallactus capensis*

A small cylindrical snake with smooth scales and small eyes. Its head is not distinct from its body. It is variable in colour, ranging from reddish-brown to grey, but the top of the head and the neck are invariably dark brown to black.

Size	To about 30 cm.
Distribution	SE Africa.
Habitat	Grasslands, scrub and mountain foothills.
Food	Centipedes.
Breeding	Egg-laying, with clutches of 2–4 eggs.
Notes	The other 10 species of centipede-eaters are similar in appearance, but this is one of the most widespread and common. A back-fanged species, but too small to be dangerous to humans.

CORPULENT BURROWING ASP *Atractaspis corpulenta*

A stocky, cylindrical snake with smooth scales and a narrow, pointed head that is not distinct from its body. Its tail is short and ends in a short spine. It is dark brown or black above, white or cream below. The long fangs can be folded back when not in use.

Size	40–50 cm.
Distribution	W Africa.
Habitat	Grassland, scrub and semi-desert regions.
Food	Other burrowing snakes and lizards, small mammals and frogs. Often uses a single fang to 'stab' its prey without fully opening its mouth.
Breeding	Egg-laying, with clutches of 3–7 eggs.
Notes	There are several other burrowing asps, all similar to look at. All are dangerous to humans, though bites are not usually fatal.

181

Cobras, Mambas, Kraits, Coral Snakes and Sea Snakes (Elapidae)

The **elapid** family, which contains an assortment of venomous snakes from most parts of the world, has almost 250 members. Although they vary in size, shape and habits, they all have a pair of fixed venom fangs at the front of their mouth. Like the colubrids, their heads are covered with large, regular shield-like scales and the scales covering their bodies are usually smooth, although a few have keeled scales.

The cobras are distinguished by their ability to spread a 'hood' by expanding the ribs in their neck region. Some of them can spit venom through small apertures at the front of each fang. The King Cobra (p.201) is the longest venomous snake in the world. Mambas are slender, tree-dwelling elapids from Africa and the kraits are slender snakes with a triangular cross-section that come from Asia.

The American coral snakes are brightly marked with bands of red, black and white or yellow, and other brightly coloured elapids from other parts of the world are also known locally as coral snakes.

The sea snakes represent a branch of the cobra family that has become totally adapted to a marine way of life. They have flattened tails for swimming, modified lungs to help them to maintain buoyancy and to dive for long periods, and special glands for disposing of excess salt. They give birth to live young. The sea kraits are almost as well adapted, but they are egg-layers and so they must come ashore occasionally.

DEATH ADDER *Acanthophis antarcticus*

A stocky snake that looks more like a viper than a typical elapid. It has a broad, triangular head, short tail and slightly keeled scales. It varies from grey to brown or red and it has a number of irregular crossbands over the body. The tip of the tail is often cream or yellow.

Size	Normally about 40–50 cm, but exceptionally to 1 m.
Distribution	Australia, except the central desert region, (see Notes).
Habitat	Dry, rocky or scrubby places.
Food	Small mammals, birds and reptiles. Sometimes uses the tip of its tail to lure prey to within striking distance.
Breeding	Live-bearing, with litters of up to 20 young.
Notes	The Desert Death Adder, *A. pyrrhus*, from central Australia, is similar. Other species occur in New Guinea. **DANGEROUSLY VENOMOUS**

AFRICAN CORAL SNAKE *Aspidelaps lubricus*

A short, stocky snake with smooth scales. A large triangular shield covers the snout. It is orange or pinkish, with a series of black crossbars. Its head is reddish, with a black line running over it and through the eyes, and there is another black bar on the neck.

Size	To about 50 cm, sometimes slightly longer.
Distribution	W parts of S Africa (the Cape region and Namibia).
Habitat	Dry grassy and rocky areas, and semi-desert.
Food	Small reptiles and possibly mammals.
Breeding	Egg-laying, with clutches of 3–11 eggs.
Notes	A second species, the Shield-nose Snake, *A. scutatus*, is rather similar in appearance, but is rare.

DANGEROUSLY VENOMOUS

AUSTRALIAN COPPERHEAD *Austrelaps superbus*

A thickset, powerful snake with large, smooth scales. It may be black, dark grey or coppery, the lowest row of scales on the flanks being larger and lighter in colour than those on the back.

Size	To about 1 m, usually rather less, but occasionally slightly more. Several 'races' grow to different lengths.
Distribution	SE Australia, and N Tasmania.
Habitat	Damp places, in mountains and lowlands.
Food	Frogs and small reptiles.
Breeding	Live-bearing, with litters of up to 20 young.
Notes	Dark specimens tend to be from highlands; the lowland populations are lighter in colour. **DANGEROUSLY VENOMOUS**

BANDED KRAIT *Bungarus fasciatus*

A moderately slender snake with a characteristic triangular cross-section to its body. Its head is narrow and barely distinct from its neck and the scales are smooth. It is patterned with alternating black and white (or cream) bands of roughly equal width, from the neck to the tip of the tail.

Size	To 2 m.
Distribution	South-east Asia.
Habitat	Forests, fields and around human habitations.
Food	Other snakes.
Breeding	Egg-laying.
Notes	The Malayan Krait, *B. candidus*, is also banded, but the bands do not go completely around the snake's body. **DANGEROUSLY VENOMOUS**

GREEN MAMBA *Dendroaspis angusticeps*

A large, elongated snake with smooth scales, a narrow, graceful head and large, dark eyes. Its head and body are uniform bright green.

Size	To about 2 m, occasionally longer.
Distribution	E Africa.
Habitat	Scrub and forested regions, where it climbs well.
Food	Birds and small mammals.
Breeding	Egg-laying, with clutches of up to 10 eggs. The young are blue-green when they first hatch.
Notes	The only plain green snake. The green snakes, *Philothamnus* (p.150), for instance, invariably have some markings. **DANGEROUSLY VENOMOUS**

BLACK MAMBA *Dendroaspis polylepis*

An elongated but powerful snake with smooth scales and a narrow head. It is not black, but often dark grey, with the texture of pewter. Some examples are brownish or olive and there are occasionally dark blotches along the back. The inside of the mouth is black.

Size	Normally to 2.5 m, but very rarely to 4.5 m.
Distribution	Most of the S half of Africa, excluding deserts.
Habitat	Grasslands and scrub.
Food	Birds and small mammals.
Breeding	Egg-laying, with clutches of 12–14 eggs.
Notes	If threatened, it may spread a narrow hood. Otherwise easily confused with other dark snakes from the region. **DANGEROUSLY VENOMOUS**

RINKHALS OR SPITTING COBRA *Hemachatus haemachatus*

A thickset snake with keeled scales and a wide head. It is varied in colour and may be marked with black bands on a grey, yellow or orange background, or it may be plain black or dark brown above, sometimes with paler speckles. It rears up and spreads a hood when alarmed.

Size	To about 1 m, occasionally slightly longer.
Distribution	S Africa.
Habitat	Grasslands.
Food	Frogs, toads, reptiles, small mammals and birds.
Breeding	Live-bearing, with litters of up to 63, but usually 20–30 young.
Notes	A spitting cobra that will spray venom accurately up to 2.5 m, aiming at the face. Attacks are painful and can cause blindness. **DANGEROUSLY VENOMOUS**

BLUE MALAYAN CORAL SNAKE *Maticora bivirgata*

A long, slender snake with smooth scales and an unusual colour and pattern. Its head and the end of the tail are orange, as is much of the underside. Its back is blue-black and the flanks are pale blue.

Size	To about 1.5 m.
Distribution	South-east Asia.
Habitat	Forests and agricultural areas.
Food	Other snakes.
Breeding	Egg-laying.
Notes	Unmistakable! Very shy and rarely seen. Normally inoffensive, but nevertheless **DANGEROUSLY VENOMOUS**

ARIZONA (OR WESTERN) CORAL SNAKE *Micruroides euryxanthus*

A slender, cylindrical snake with smooth scales, a small head that is barely distinct from its neck, and small eyes. It is patterned with alternating rings of red, white and black; the red bands are always bordered on each side by white ones (black–white–red–white–black, etc.)

Size	To about 50 cm.
Distribution	S Arizona and adjacent parts of Sonora, Mexico.
Habitat	Dry places, including deserts, scrub and grassland.
Food	Lizards and snakes, especially burrowing kinds.
Breeding	Egg-laying. Thought to produce clutches of 2–3 eggs.
Notes	Harmless kingsnakes and milksnakes have red bands bordered by black ones. Other tri-coloured snakes have light-coloured snouts. **DANGEROUSLY VENOMOUS**

191

SOUTHERN CORAL SNAKE *Micrurus frontalis*

A slender, cylindrical snake with smooth scales and small eyes. This species has an unusual arrangement of bands, with a double white band between the red ones, so that the sequence is red–black–white–black–white–black–red and so on.

Size	To about 1 m.
Distribution	South America, from central Brazil to S Argentina. The most southerly species of coral snake.
Habitat	Tropical and cooler forests, farmland and grassland.
Food	Other reptiles.
Breeding	Egg-laying.
Notes	There are about 50 other species of coral snakes in Central and South America and they all look rather similar. Species identification may require an expert. All are **DANGEROUSLY VENOMOUS**

TEXAS CORAL SNAKE *Micrurus fulvius*

A slender snake with smooth, shiny scales. It has a black snout, behind which is a wide yellow band across the head. The rest of the body is marked with wide red and black bands, separated from one another by narrow yellow ones.

Size	To about 75 cm.
Distribution	SE USA and adjacent parts of Mexico.
Habitat	Dry or moist areas, often with sandy soil. Secretive; hides under logs and in stumps.
Food	Other snakes, lizards and frogs.
Breeding	Egg-laying, with clutches of 3–5 eggs.
Notes	Kingsnakes and milksnakes have red and black bands touching. **DANGEROUSLY VENOMOUS**

SOUTH AMERICAN CORAL SNAKE *Micrurus lemniscatus*

A very slender snake, with smooth scales, a small head and small eyes. It is patterned with wide red bands, separated by an equally wide combination of black–white–black–white–black. It has a white bar just behind the snout, a black bar passing through the eyes, and its neck is red.

Size	To about 1 m, but occasionally to 1.5 m.
Distribution	N South America, Trinidad and Tobago.
Habitat	Rain forests and plantations, etc.
Food	Other snakes and lizards.
Breeding	Egg-laying.
Notes	See notes for Southern Coral Snake (p.192).
	DANGEROUSLY VENOMOUS

FOREST COBRA *Naja melanoleuca*

A slender cobra with smooth, shiny scales. Its head and the front of its body are greyish-brown, speckled with black. The lower half of its body is glossy black. It rears up and spreads a narrow hood when it is alarmed.

Size	To about 2 m, occasionally longer.
Distribution	Tropical and subtropical Africa.
Habitat	Rain forests.
Food	Frogs and toads, lizards, snakes, birds and small mammals.
Breeding	Egg-laying, with clutches of 15–26 eggs.
Notes	The largest African cobra. The only species with the lower part of the body and tail darker than the front half. **DANGEROUSLY VENOMOUS**

MOZAMBIQUE SPITTING COBRA *Naja mossambica*

Moderately slender, with smooth scales and a blunt snout. It is light grey to olive-brown and each scale is edged in black. It is yellow or pinkish below and there are several dark blotches or crossbars on the throat. When alarmed, it spreads a broad hood and may spit venom.

Size	To about 1.2 m, occasionally longer.
Distribution	E and S Africa.
Habitat	Grasslands and forest clearings.
Food	Toads, lizards and small mammals. Also grasshoppers.
Breeding	Egg-laying, with clutches of 10–22 eggs.
Notes	Other African spitters include the Rinkhals (p.189) and the Black-necked Cobra, *N. nigricollis*, which is uniform black or has a black throat.

DANGEROUSLY VENOMOUS

INDIAN (OR SPECTACLED) COBRA *Naja naja*

A slender snake with smooth scales. It is variable in colour, but is usually black or dark brown above with lighter markings on the throat. It spreads a very wide hood when alarmed and may display a bold white marking, in the shape of a 'spectacle', on the back.

Size	To 2 m, but usually less.
Distribution	India, Pakistan and Sri Lanka.
Habitat	Forests, farmland and around towns and villages.
Food	Other reptiles, small mammals.
Breeding	Egg-laying.
Notes	There are other cobras in Asia, but only this one has the spectacle marking on the back of the hood. **DANGEROUSLY VENOMOUS**

INDONESIAN SPITTING COBRA *Naja sputatrix*

A stocky snake with smooth scales and a broad head. It is uniform black, brown or dark grey, with some obscure pale areas on the underside of the hood, but none on its back. It spits venom through small apertures in its fangs.

Size	To about 2 m.
Distribution	Malaysian peninsula and the larger Indonesian islands.
Habitat	Forests, farmlands and villages.
Food	Frogs, lizards, snakes and rodents.
Breeding	Egg-laying.
Notes	Used to be classed with the Indian Cobra (p.197), as were several other similar Asian cobras that are now regarded as separate species. **DANGEROUSLY VENOMOUS**

BLACK TIGER SNAKE *Notechis ater*

A chunky snake with large, shiny scales and a broad head. Usually jet black, although it sometimes has traces of lighter crossbands. It may spread its neck when alarmed, although it cannot form a hood.

Size	To about 1 m, but larger on some islands.
Distribution	Australia: Tasmania, islands in the Bass Strait, SW Australia and islands along the S coast.
Habitat	Rocky places, tussock grass, dunes and beaches.
Food	Frogs, small mammals and seabird chicks on some islands.
Breeding	Live-bearing.
Notes	Some islands have unusual populations, such as giant or dwarf forms. Its range does not overlap with the other Tiger Snake (p.200). **DANGEROUSLY VENOMOUS**

TIGER SNAKE *Notechis scutatus*

A slender snake with smooth scales. It can be grey, olive or even reddish and usually has a series of lighter crossbands that can be difficult to make out. It flattens its neck when it is angry, although it is normally a fairly placid snake.

Size	To 1.2 m.
Distribution	SE Australia.
Habitat	Forests and open grasslands.
Food	Mainly frogs.
Breeding	Live-bearing, with litters of up to 100 or more young, but usually about 30.
Notes	A fairly distinctive species.
	DANGEROUSLY VENOMOUS

KING COBRA *Ophiophagus hannah*

A large and impressive snake, but quite slender. The adult is olive with black edges to the scales. The young are dark brown or black with many narrow, chevron-shaped bands of white or yellow. It rears up and spreads a narrow hood when it is aroused.

Size	To 5.5 m, making it the longest venomous snake in the world, by far.
Distribution	India, S China, South-east Asia and the Philippines.
Habitat	Forests, foothills and open, cultivated regions.
Food	Other snakes (*Ophiophagus* means 'snake-eating').
Breeding	Egg-laying, with clutches of 20–40 eggs, which are laid in a nest of leaves and guarded by the female (maybe also the male) until they hatch.
Notes	Unmistakable due to its large size. Not aggressive, although **EXTREMELY VENOMOUS**

INLAND TAIPAN OR FIERCE SNAKE *Oxyuranus microlepidotus*

A slender and graceful snake with smooth scales and large, dark eyes. It is brown or olive, sometimes with scattered black markings on the head or, sometimes, with a uniformly black head. It does not have a hood, but may raise the front of its body off the ground when disturbed.

Size	To about 2 m, occasionally slightly more.
Distribution	Central Australia.
Habitat	Dry plains and grasslands.
Food	Small mammals.
Breeding	Egg-laying, with clutches of 12–20 eggs.
Notes	Among the most dangerous snakes in the world, although rare. Similar to the Taipan (opposite), but from a different part of Australia.

DANGEROUSLY VENOMOUS

TAIPAN *Oxyuranus scutellatus*

A long, slender snake with smooth or lightly keeled scales. It may be light or dark brown, fading to a paler shade on the sides and underside. Its head is usually lighter in colour, sometimes cream.

Size	To about 2 m.
Distribution	NE and extreme N Australia, and New Guinea.
Habitat	Forests, open woodlands and lightly wooded grasslands. Found on the ground and active mainly by day and in the evening.
Food	Small mammals.
Breeding	Egg-laying, with clutches of 2–20 eggs.
Notes	One of the most venomous snakes in the world. Fortunately, it is quite rare and secretive. Similar to the Inland Taipan (opposite), but usually darker. **DANGEROUSLY VENOMOUS**

KING BROWN SNAKE OR MULGA *Pseudechis australis*

A stocky snake with a broad head. It may be mid-brown, dark reddish-brown or dark olive and each scale may have a black border or a black tip. The colour becomes paler on the sides and the underside is cream or pinkish.

Size	To 2 m.
Distribution	The whole of Australia except extreme S.
Habitat	Very adapatable: from rain forests to deserts. May be active by day or night, depending on climate.
Food	Frogs, other reptiles and small mammals.
Breeding	Live-bearing, with litters of about 12 young.
Notes	Among the commonest Australian snakes over much of its range. Related and similar species have more restricted ranges. **DANGEROUSLY VENOMOUS**

WESTERN BROWN SNAKE *Pseudonaja nuchalis*

A slender, whip-like snake with a narrow head. Highly variable in colour, it may be light brown to black and it may be a uniform colour or have a series of lighter bands around the body, a black head and neck or many narrow dark crossbars. Combinations of these markings are also possible.

Size	To 1.5 m.
Distribution	Most of Australia except the extreme SW and SE.
Habitat	Varied, from forests to grasslands, gravelly plains and deserts.
Food	Small mammals and reptiles.
Breeding	Egg-laying.
Notes	Extreme variability can make this snake hard to identify without close examination.
	DANGEROUSLY VENOMOUS

AUSTRALIAN CORAL SNAKE *Simoselaps australis*

A small snake with smooth, shiny scales and a pointed and slightly upturned snout. It is pink or red with a series of irregular crossbars of cream-centred, dark brown scales. There is a wide black band across the head and another on the neck.

Size	To about 30 cm, sometimes slightly longer.
Distribution	E parts of Australia, but patchy.
Habitat	Forests, light woodland and scrub. A burrowing snake, usually under logs in the day or on the surface at night.
Food	Lizards.
Breeding	Egg-laying with clutches of 4–6 eggs.
Notes	This and similar species of *Simoselaps*, are sometimes called Shovel-nosed snakes. **VENOMOUS**, but docile and too small to be dangerous.

BANDY-BANDY *Vermicella annulata*

A long and slender snake with smooth scales, a narrow head and small eyes. Its coloration is very distinctive: it is mainly black with about 30 wide white rings around the body and tail, with the first band passing across the top of the head.

Size	To about 60 cm.
Distribution	Most of Australia, except the SW.
Habitat	Forests, lightly wooded grasslands and scrub, usually with sandy soil. A burrowing snake, found on the surface only at night.
Food	Thought to feed only on blind snakes.
Breeding	Egg-laying.
Notes	A similar species, *V. multifasciata*, has narrower white bands and is rare and very poorly known. **VENOMOUS**, but too small to be dangerous.

DESERT BLACK SNAKE *Walterinnesia aegyptia*

A moderately slender snake with smooth, shiny scales and small eyes. It is usually black or very dark grey and does not spread a hood.

Size	To about 1 m.
Distribution	Egypt, parts of the Arabian peninsula and the Middle East.
Habitat	Deserts and rocky places. Also in parks and on waste ground near towns and villages.
Food	Small mammals, birds and lizards.
Breeding	Thought to be an egg-layer.
Notes	A distinctive cobra, but sometimes confused with the harmless Large Whipsnake (p.88), with which it shares some of its range. **DANGEROUSLY VENOMOUS**

VIPERS AND PIT VIPERS (VIPERIDAE)

The vipers represent the pinnacle of snake evolution and have a number of features that are not found in other families. They have long fangs attached to a small hinged bone, so they can be folded out of the way when not in use. They have large venom glands, which tend to give their heads a broad, triangular shape. Although they produce large quantities of venom, it is not as toxic, weight for weight, as that of the cobra family. It contains several components, but often acts on the blood and blood vessels causing haemorrhage and tissue damage, which can be severe or even fatal in the case of bites from the most dangerous species.

One group of vipers, popularly known as 'pit vipers', have a pair of specialised sense organs in their face, which they use to pick up infrared radiation (heat) coming from potential prey (see also p.9). Pit vipers are found in North and South America and in parts of Asia. The rattlesnakes, which form a subdivision of the pit vipers, are well known, and instantly recognisable, because of the rattle that forms the end of their tail and with which they warn potential enemies to keep their distance. Rattlesnakes are found only in North and South America. Other vipers are found in Europe and Africa, but they are completely absent from the Australian region and Madagascar.

The typical vipers are described first, followed by the pit vipers.

HAIRY BUSH VIPER *Atheris hispida*

A slender viper with extremely elongated scales that are heavily keeled and curl up at the tips, making the snake appear spiky and giving it its common name. It is usually pale to dark green, but it may also be yellowish. There may be a number of faint, ill-defined crossbars along the back.

Size	To about 60 cm.
Distribution	W Africa.
Habitat	Forests, where it is found only in trees.
Food	Frogs, lizards and, probably, small mammals.
Breeding	Live-bearing.
Notes	The upturned scales, expecially on the neck, make this an unmistakable species. **DANGEROUSLY VENOMOUS**

SEDGE VIPER *Atheris nitschei*

A stocky snake with heavily keeled scales. It has large eyes with vertical pupils. Adults are bright green with black markings down the centre of the back and on the head. Juveniles are dark grey with hardly any markings, but with a cream tip to the tail.

Size	To about 60 cm.
Distribution	E and Central Africa.
Habitat	Rain forests.
Food	Frogs, lizards and small rodents.
Breeding	Live-bearing, with clutches of up to 10 young.
Notes	This species and its relatives closely parallel the South American pit vipers such as the Eyelash Viper (p.234). **DANGEROUSLY VENOMOUS**

PUFF ADDER *Bitis arietans*

A large and bulky snake with a wide, flat, triangular head. Its scales are heavily keeled and the tail is very short. It is brown or yellowish, with black chevron-shaped markings down the back. Each chevron has a white trailing edge. The markings are sometimes confused and poorly defined.

Size	To about 1 m.
Distribution	Throughout Africa.
Habitat	Very generalised; in most habitats except deserts.
Food	Small mammals and birds.
Breeding	Live-bearing, with recorded litters of over 100 young, but more usually 20–40.
Notes	Not similar to any other African viper or adder. **DANGEROUSLY VENOMOUS**

HORNED ADDER *Bitis caudalis*

A short, stocky snake with a flattened body and short tail. Its scales are heavily keeled and it has a small horn above each eye. Its colour varies greatly with the soil on which it lives, and may be grey, tan, reddish or brown, with a series of darker blotches down the back and alternating blotches on each flank.

Size	To about 40 cm.
Distribution	S and SW Africa.
Habitat	Scrub, semi-desert and true desert regions.
Food	Small lizards, rodents and frogs.
Breeding	Live-bearing, with litters of 4–15 young, maybe more.
Notes	There are several other small desert adders in the region. The single horn is a good feature; others have either a cluster of small horns or none at all. **VENOMOUS**

MANY-HORNED VIPER *Bitis cornuta*

A thickset viper with keeled scales and a cluster of 2, 3 or 4 horns over each eye. It is greyish-brown with four rows of pale-edged, dark brown irregular blotches along the back. It has a dark, pointed marking on the top of the head.

Size	To about 50 cm.
Distribution	S Africa.
Habitat	Sandy and rocky places.
Food	Lizards, rodents and amphibians.
Breeding	Live-bearing, with litters of up to 20 small young.
Notes	Specimens from the south of the range may lack the horns. Otherwise easy to identify. **VENOMOUS**

GABOON VIPER *Bitis gabonica*

An incredibly large and heavy-bodied snake with a broad, flat, triangular head, small eyes and a short tail. Its colours and markings defy description, having a geometric design of rectangles, triangles and diamonds of buff, purple, pink and various shades of brown. Light and dark lines radiate from the eye.

Size	To about 1.2 m, very rarely approaching 2 m.
Distribution	Central and E Africa.
Habitat	Forests, where it lives on the ground. Its pattern provides excellent camouflage among leaf-litter.
Food	Small and medium-sized mammals and birds.
Breeding	Live-bearing, with litters of up to 60 young.
Notes	An unmistakable snake – once seen never forgotten! **DANGEROUSLY VENOMOUS**

RHINOCEROS VIPER *Bitis nasicornis*

A stocky snake with heavily keeled scales and a strange cluster of enlarged, horn-like scales on the snout. Its colours and patterns are intricate, with a row of bluish-green, bow-tie-shaped markings on a deep purplish-brown background. Its flanks are paler and the markings are often edged in yellow.

Size	To about 1 m.
Distribution	W Africa.
Habitat	Forests, especially along riverbanks.
Food	Small mammals and birds.
Breeding	Live-bearing.
Notes	A bizarre but beautiful viper that is unlike any other species. **DANGEROUSLY VENOMOUS**

Peringuey's Viper *Bitis peringueyi*

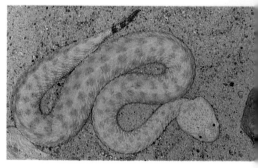

A small, stocky viper with heavily keeled scales. Its head is rounded and flattened and its eyes are situated on top, looking straight up. It can be light brown, fawn, creamy-grey or pinkish with three rows of faint spots running down the back. Moves by sidewinding.

Size	To about 25 cm.
Distribution	A narrow coastal strip of suitable habitat in Namibia.
Habitat	Wind-blown sand-dunes in the Namib Desert.
Food	Small lizards.
Breeding	Live-bearing, with litters of 3–10 young.
Notes	There are other small vipers in the region, but none are so well adapted to living in loose sand. **VENOMOUS**

SPOTTED NIGHT ADDER *Causus maculatus*

A medium-sized snake with weakly keeled scales, a rounded snout and round pupils. All night adders have large plates on top of their heads. It is grey or greenish with faint blotches along its back.

Size	To about 75 cm.
Distribution	Central Africa.
Habitat	Grasslands and lightly wooded areas.
Food	Amphibians, especially toads.
Breeding	Egg-laying.
Notes	There are 5 other species of night adders in Africa. Their venom is quite weak, causing only localised pain. **VENOMOUS**

DESERT HORNED VIPER *Cerastes cerastes*

A fairly slender viper with roughly keeled scales and a broad head. It usually has a single, long, thorn-like scale over each eye, but these may be lacking at times. It is sandy, buff, light grey or pinkish and often has a row, or two parallel rows, of large darker blotches down the back. It moves by sidewinding and rubs its scales together to make a loud rasping sound when annoyed.

Size	To about 60 cm.
Distribution	N Africa.
Habitat	Dunes and other areas of loose, wind-blown sand.
Food	Lizards and small mammals.
Breeding	Egg-laying, with clutches of up to 20 eggs.
Notes	There are 2 other species, one of which also has horns, but this is the most common. **VENOMOUS**

CARPET (OR SAW-SCALED) VIPER *Echis carinatus*

Quite a slender viper, with variable markings. It is often grey or brown with a darker area along the centre of the back, in which there are a number of small white spots. It has specialised scales on its sides, which it rubs together to produce a rasping sound.

Size	To about 75 cm.
Distribution	From W Africa to India and Sri Lanka (but see Notes).
Habitat	Deserts, scrub and arid grasslands.
Food	Lizards and small mammals.
Breeding	Live-bearing.
Notes	Will shortly be divided into 5 or 6 similar species. There are also 2 further species, similar in appearance, from the Middle East. **DANGEROUSLY VENOMOUS** and responsible for many deaths.

MILOS VIPER *Macrovipera schweizeri*

A chunky viper with a blunt nose and keeled scales. It is usually grey with faint crossbands of darker grey or pale orange. Its face is mottled with fine dark markings. A few specimens are uniform reddish-brown.

Size	To 1 m.
Distribution	The Greek islands of Milos, Kimilos, Syphnos and Polyagos.
Habitat	Dry, rocky, scrub-covered valleys and hillsides.
Food	Mainly birds, also small mammals.
Breeding	Egg-laying.
Notes	Sometimes regarded as a form of the Blunt-nosed Viper, *M. lebetina*, which has a wider range in W Asia. **DANGEROUSLY VENOMOUS**

NOSE-HORNED VIPER *Vipera ammodytes*

A large viper with keeled scales and a conspicuous fleshy horn on the tip of the snout. It is silver grey, brown or orange with a zigzag marking in a darker shade. The centre of the zigzag may be lighter than the edges and it may be broken into a number of separate blotches.

Size	To about 1 m.
Distribution	SE Europe, all of Turkey, and adjacent parts of neighbouring countries.
Habitat	Dry, rocky places. Also drystone walls and meadows.
Food	Small mammals and birds.
Breeding	Live-bearing, with litters of up to 10 young.
Notes	Look for the prominent upturned snout. **DANGEROUSLY VENOMOUS**

ASPIC VIPER *Vipera aspis*

A rather slender viper with keeled scales, a broad head and an upturned snout (but no horn). It is usually light brown, grey or cream, but the markings are variable: it may have a wavy zigzag (often with a paler centre) or a series of short dark crossbars down the back, joined with a thin central line. Sometimes it is uniformly black.

Size	To about 60 cm, occasionally longer.
Distribution	Central Europe and Italy.
Habitat	Dry hillsides, mountains, meadows, etc.
Food	Small mammals and lizards.
Breeding	Live-bearing.
Notes	Easily confused with the Adder (p.226), but distinguished by the raised snout. **VENOMOUS**, but fatal bites are rare.

ADDER *Vipera berus*

A fairly thick-bodied viper with a few large scales on the top of the head and keeled scales on the body. Males are grey with a dark grey or black zigzag down the back; females are usually brown or reddish with a dark brown zigzag. Some adders are plain black.

Size	To about 70 cm, occasionally longer.
Distribution	N, W and central Europe (including Britain and Scandinavia), central and E Asia. Has the largest range of any land snake.
Habitat	Heaths, bogs, woods, fields etc. Active by day.
Food	Lizards and small rodents.
Breeding	Live-bearing, with litters of up to 10 young.
Notes	The only viper in much of its range, and the one with the most regular zigzag in other places. **VENOMOUS**, but fatal bites are rare.

LATASTE'S VIPER *Vipera latasti*

A stout viper with keeled scales and a fleshy horn on the snout. It is grey or pale brown with a wavy zigzag down the back; this marking is often paler in the centre than on the edges. It also has a row of dark blotches along each flank.

Size	To about 60 cm.
Distribution	Spain and Portugal, except the N coast, and NW Africa.
Habitat	Dry, stony hillsides or sandy areas near the coast (in S Spain).
Food	Small mammals, birds and lizards.
Breeding	Live-bearing.
Notes	The only Spanish viper with a horn on the snout and the only viper over most of its range. **VENOMOUS**

PALESTINE VIPER *Vipera palaestinae*

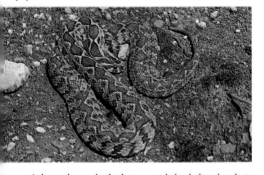

A large, heavy-bodied viper with keeled scales. It is usually grey, light brown or orange-brown and has a broad, dark brown or black wavy-edged line along the back. Two broad dark lines radiate out from the eyes and another crosses the snout.

Size	To 1.3 m.
Distribution	Middle East.
Habitat	Dry sandy areas.
Food	Small mammals.
Breeding	Egg-laying, with clutches of up to 20 eggs.
Notes	By far the largest viper in its area.
	DANGEROUSLY VENOMOUS

RUSSELL'S VIPER *Vipera russelli*

A large, bulky viper, though not especially stout. It is pale greyish-brown with a number of dark brown, white-edged ovals along the back, which are often partly joined together. Another series of ovals runs down each flank, alternating with those on the back. Several dark wedge-shaped marks radiate out from the eyes.

Size To about 1 m, sometimes longer.
Distribution India, Burma, Pakistan and Sri Lanka.
Habitat Grasslands, scrub, plantations.
Food Small mammals.
Breeding Live-bearing, with litters of up to 65 young.
Notes Very distinctive and the only large viper in the Indian region. Sometimes placed in the genus *Daboia*.
DANGEROUSLY VENOMOUS

CANTIL *Agkistrodon bilineatus*

A thick-bodied pit viper with a relatively long tail. Its head is triangular and has a thin white line running from the tip of its snout along its upper jaw and another through its eyes. Its body is black or dark brown with wide bands of slightly paler brown edged with white.

Size	To about 1 m.
Distribution	W coast of Mexico.
Habitat	Dry forests and scrub.
Food	Rodents, and probably lizards.
Breeding	Live-bearing, with litters of up to 10 young.
Notes	The thin white lines on its head make this one of the most distinctive pit vipers. **DANGEROUSLY VENOMOUS**

COPPERHEAD *Agkistrodon contortrix*

A stout snake with weakly keeled scales and a triangular head. Its pattern has bands of tan, buff or pink alternating with bands of dark red or chestnut brown. The bands are equally wide, but darker ones may become wider on the flanks. The tip of the tail may be yellow, especially in young snakes.

Size	To about 75 cm.
Distribution	SE USA, except Florida, and NE Mexico.
Habitat	Rocky hillsides, swamps and desert oases, depending on locality.
Food	Rodents, small birds and frogs.
Breeding	Live-bearing, with litters of up to 8 young.
Notes	Easily confused with some water snakes, but these have strongly keeled scales and lack the facial pit. **VENOMOUS**

231

COTTONMOUTH *Agkistrodon piscivorus*

A large, chunky snake with weakly keeled scales. It is brown, dark grey or black with obscure crossbands that are often hard to make out. There is sometimes (especially in Florida) a thin white line passing from the snout and above the eye.

Size	To about 1.25 m, occasionally to 1.75 m.
Distribution	SE USA.
Habitat	Swamps, lakes, rivers and ditches.
Food	Fish, frogs, salamanders, other reptiles (including turtles), birds and small mammals. It also scavenges.
Breeding	Live-bearing, with litters of 3–12 large young.
Notes	Easily confused with several species of water snake. Thick-bodied, dark-coloured, semi-aquatic snakes from this part of the world are best left alone! **DANGEROUSLY VENOMOUS** and bad-tempered.

STRIPED PALM VIPER *Bothriechis lateralis*

A slender pit viper with keeled scales and an outstandingly beautiful colour scheme. Its head and body are bluish-green with a small number of white spots or crossbars along the back. The young are brown with black and white markings and they first change to green before taking on the adult coloration.

Size	About 70 cm, occasionally to 1 m.
Distribution	Costa Rica and Panama, in Central America.
Habitat	Tropical forests, where is it always found in trees.
Food	Probably lizards, frogs and occasional small mammals and birds.
Breeding	Live-bearing.
Notes	There are other bluish-green pit vipers in the region and identification can be difficult.

DANGEROUSLY VENOMOUS

EYELASH VIPER *Bothriopsis schlegelii*

A slender pit viper with heavily keeled scales and a prehensile tail. It is instantly recognisable due to its 'eyelashes', a cluster of small spine-like scales over each eye. It varies in colour and may be uniform yellow, or green with brown blotches and mottled black and brown flecks, resembling lichen.

Size	To about 60 cm, occasionally to 80 cm.
Distribution	Central and South America, from S Mexico to N Colombia.
Habitat	Tropical rain and cloud forests, where it lives in trees.
Food	Lizards, small birds and mammals.
Breeding	Live-bearing.
Notes	An unusual and unmistakable species. **VENOMOUS**

FER-DE-LANCE *Bothrops atrox*

A fairly stout snake with keeled scales and a sharply pointed snout. It is brownish or grey with indistinct markings of dark blotches and light streaks, irregularly arranged or formed into vague crossbars. It always has a dark streak running from each eye to the angle of the jaw.

Size	To about 1.5 m.
Distribution	N part of the Amazon Basin, South America.
Habitat	Tropical forests, usually in moist places and often near streams and rivers.
Food	Small mammals and lizards.
Breeding	Live-bearing.
Notes	There are several similar species which can be hard to distinguish. **DANGEROUSLY VENOMOUS**

EASTERN DIAMONDBACK RATTLESNAKE *Crotalus adamanteus*

A large, bulky rattlesnake with a broad, rounded head. It may be brown or olive with large diamonds of dark brown along the back. Each diamond is outlined with light-coloured scales and there may be smaller dark blotches between the diamonds. It has two light-coloured streaks on the face.

Size   Usually to about 1.7 m, but recorded up to 2.4 m.
Distribution   Florida, and coastal parts of nearby states.
Habitat   Pinewoods and palm scrub.
Food   Small mammals, including rabbits, and birds.
Breeding   Live-bearing.
Notes   The largest rattler in the E USA and the only one with two light streaks on the face.
DANGEROUSLY VENOMOUS

WESTERN DIAMONDBACK RATTLESNAKE *Crotalus atrox* ☠

A large rattler with a rounded snout. Its colour varies and may be grey, bluish, pink or black. It has a series of large, light-edged diamonds running down the back, although these can be hard to make out, and smaller blotches on the flanks. It has two light streaks on the face, with a darker area in between.

Size	To about 1.7 m, but sometimes over 2 m.
Distribution	Much of SW USA, E to Texas, and N Mexico.
Habitat	Dry desert, scrub and grasslands.
Food	Rabbits, squirrels, other rodents and birds.
Breeding	Live-bearing, with litters of up to 40 young.
Notes	Look for the wide black and white bands in front of the rattle on the tail. A very common species. **DANGEROUSLY VENOMOUS**

SIDEWINDER *Crotalus cerastes*

A small, fairly slender rattlesnake with a horn-like scale above each eye. Its colour matches the sand on which it lives, and may be yellow, tan, buff, grey or pink, and it has a row of blotches down the back. Its name reflects the way it moves sideways across loose sand.

Size	To about 75 cm.
Distribution	SW USA and NW Mexico in suitable habitat.
Habitat	Only where there are dunes and sizeable areas of loose, wind-blown sand. Shuffles down beneath the surface during the day.
Food	Lizards and small mice.
Breeding	Live-bearing, with litters of 5–18 young.
Notes	Unmistakable, but similar to desert vipers from other parts of the world. **VENOMOUS** and often aggressive if disturbed.

SOUTH AMERICAN RATTLESNAKE *Crotalus durissus*

A stout rattlesnake with several different races, which vary in colour and markings. It ranges from light grey, through brown, yellow and tan, to greenish-grey, olive and black. Many subspecies are marked with a series of diamonds along the back, typically darker than the background and edged in white or yellow. The picture shows subspecies *vegrandis*.

Size	To about 1.5 m, occasionally slightly longer.
Distribution	From Mexico to Argentina.
Habitat	Dry forests, scrub and grasslands. Not rain forests.
Food	Mammals and birds.
Breeding	Live-bearing.
Notes	The only rattlesnake over much of South America. Look for a pair of parallel lines on the neck. **DANGEROUSLY VENOMOUS**

CANEBRAKE RATTLESNAKE *Crotalus horridus atricaudatus*

A stout rattlesnake with a distinctive colour pattern. It is mainly brownish-grey, with a number of very dark bars or chevrons along the back. It has an orange or cinnamon stripe along the centre of the back, interrupted by the chevrons. It becomes darker towards the tail, which may be nearly black.

Size	To about 1.3 m, occasionally to nearly 2 m.
Distribution	E half of the USA, except the Florida peninsula.
Habitat	Wooded valleys and lowland thickets.
Food	Rodents and birds.
Breeding	Live-bearing, with litters of about 10 young.
Notes	The Timber Rattlesnake, *C. h. horridus*, is yellowish and lacks the central stripe. Both are **DANGEROUSLY VENOMOUS**

BANDED ROCK RATTLESNAKE *Crotalus lepidus*

A medium-sized rattlesnake with a variety of colours and markings. It is commonly grey, with a number of wide dark bands across the body. The background may also be greenish-grey (especially in males), and the bands may be brown or faded grey. The spaces between the bands may be speckled with dark spots.

Size	To about 60 cm.
Distribution	S USA (Texas, New Mexico and Arizona) and much of N-central Mexico.
Habitat	Dry, lightly wooded places, among rocks and scree.
Food	Small mammals, snakes, lizards and frogs.
Breeding	Live-bearing, with litters of 2–8 young.
Notes	The boldly banded type is the most common form and is quite distinct from other rattlesnakes. **VENOMOUS** and often bad-tempered.

BLACK-TAILED RATTLESNAKE *Crotalus molossus*

Quite a large rattlesnake with a variable pattern. It is often greenish, but may also be yellow, tan, orange or brown. It has a series of diamonds along the back, but these are sometimes irregular and hard to make out. Its tail is black, and it usually has a black 'mask' over the face, although this is sometimes lacking.

Size	To about 1 m.
Distribution	S-central USA and central Mexico.
Habitat	Scrub, semi-desert and dry, lightly wooded places.
Food	Small mammals and birds. Possibly also lizards.
Breeding	Live-bearing, with litters of 3–6 young.
Notes	The black tail and black face marking are distinctive. Normally a very placid species, but nevertheless **DANGEROUSLY VENOMOUS**

RED DIAMOND RATTLESNAKE *Crotalus ruber*

A large rattlesnake with quite a slender body. It is brick-red, pale reddish-brown or orange. The large diamonds along the centre of the back are slightly darker than the background and are edged with paler scales, especially on the front half of the body. Its tail has narrow black and white rings in front of the rattle.

Size	To about 1 m, occasionally up to 1.5 m.
Distribution	S California and Baja California, Mexico.
Habitat	Deserts.
Food	Small mammals and birds.
Breeding	Live-bearing, with litters of 3–20 young.
Notes	The only distinctly reddish rattlesnake. Normally a placid species, but **DANGEROUSLY VENOMOUS**

MOJAVE RATTLESNAKE *Crotalus scutulatus*

A medium-sized rattlesnake that is easily confused with other species. It is greenish-grey or brown with a series of oval or diamond-shaped markings along the back. There is usually a light-coloured stripe from the eye to the corner of the mouth.

Size	To about 1 m, but occasionally slightly longer.
Distribution	SW USA and well into central Mexico.
Habitat	Deserts, dry scrub and lightly wooded, rocky areas.
Food	Small mammals.
Breeding	Live-bearing, with litters of 2–11 young.
Notes	Identification can be hard – look for the banded tail, with wide white and narrow black rings. An **EXTREMELY DANGEROUS** rattlesnake; bad-tempered, with very potent venom.

TIGER RATTLESNAKE *Crotalus tigris*

A heavy-bodied and attractively marked rattlesnake with a distinctive pattern. It may be grey, pinkish or lavender, with faint crossbands of a darker shade. It has a relatively small head and large rattle.

Size	To about 85 cm.
Distribution	S Arizona and Sonora State, Mexico.
Habitat	Rocky canyons and hillsides, often where cactus are plentiful.
Food	Small mammals.
Breeding	Live-bearing.
Notes	Uncommon. More subtle coloration than most rattlesnakes. Has a calm disposition, but **DANGEROUSLY VENOMOUS**

WESTERN RATTLESNAKE *Crotalus viridis*

A highly variable species with several regional forms. It invariably has a row of dark blotches along the back, which may be olive, brown or black. Its background can be grey, cream, light green or buff, and the blotches can be difficult to make out on dark individuals.

Size	To about 1.5 m, but often smaller.
Distribution	Almost the whole of W USA, extending into extreme N Mexico.
Habitat	Prairies, desert foothills, forests.
Food	Small mammals, birds and other reptiles.
Breeding	Live-bearing, with litters of up to 25.
Notes	Boldly blotched, or very dark (in Arizona) rattlesnakes are usually this species. **DANGEROUSLY VENOMOUS**

BUSHMASTER *Lachesis muta*

A large and magnificent pit viper, built like a rattlesnake, but lacking the rattle. It is light brown, yellowish or tan with a row of diamond-shaped blotches along the back. Each blotch may have two pale triangles within it, on either side of the midline. It has a dark stripe from the eye to the angle of the jaw.

Size	Often to 2 m, occasionally over 3 m.
Distribution	Lower Central America and N South America.
Habitat	Lowland rain forests.
Food	Small mammals.
Breeding	Egg-laying, with clutches of about 10 eggs.
Notes	The heavily keeled scales and large size should make it easy to identify. Not normally aggressive, but nevertheless **DANGEROUSLY VENOMOUS**

MASSASSAUGA *Sistrurus catenatus*

A small rattlesnake with a tiny rattle. It has large plates on the top of the head, unlike rattlesnakes of the genus *Crotalus*. It is dark grey with a row of dark brown, elongated blotches along the back. It has a wide stripe from the snout to the back of the head.

Size	To about 75 cm.
Distribution	It has a limited range in E-central USA (Great Lakes to S Texas) and adjacent parts of N Mexico.
Habitat	Damp places, including swamps and river beds. Also grasslands and lightly wooded places. Becoming rare.
Food	Small mammals, lizards, snakes and frogs.
Breeding	Live-bearing, with litters of up to 20 young.
Notes	The small rattle and large scales on top of the head are unique, except for the Pygmy Rattlesnake (opposite) whose range is separate. **VENOMOUS**

PYGMY RATTLESNAKE *Sistrurus miliarius*

A small rattlesnake with a minute rattle and large scales on its head. It is brown, light grey or pinkish, and may have a brick-red line down the centre of the back. Its other markings are a row of dark blotches along the back, and smaller dark blotches on the flanks.

Size	To about 50 cm.
Distribution	SE USA.
Habitat	Pinewoods, scrub and swampy places. Often on sandy soil.
Food	Mice, lizards, snakes and frogs.
Breeding	Live-bearing, with litters of up to 10 young.
Notes	The tiny rattle, producing a soft buzzing sound, is the best identification guide. **VENOMOUS**

WHITE-LIPPED PIT VIPER *Trimeresurus albolabris*

A thick-bodied tree viper with a deep head and conspicuous orange eyes with vertical pupils. It is pale green above, yellowish-green below. Males have a thin white line running along each flank, but this is absent in females.

Size	To about 70 cm.
Distribution	NE India to SE China.
Habitat	Forests, where it lives in trees.
Food	Lizards, frogs and rodents.
Breeding	Live-bearing.
Notes	There are several other predominantly green pit vipers from Asia. This species is frequently seen in zoos. **DANGEROUSLY VENOMOUS**

POPE'S PIT VIPER *Trimeresurus popeorum*

A slender viper with a large, triangular head and weakly keeled scales. It is uniformly green, except for the tail, which is red or reddish-brown. Young snakes have a pale line, bordered by a red line, along the flanks and the pale line may be present in adults.

Size	To about 90 cm.
Distribution	N India and South-east Asia.
Habitat	Forests, especially in small trees and shrubs in hills and mountains.
Food	Lizards, frogs and small mammals.
Breeding	Live-bearing.
Notes	This is the largest of the green pit vipers from Asia. **DANGEROUSLY VENOMOUS**

WAGLER'S PIT VIPER *Tropidolaemus wagleri*

A bulky pit viper with distinctive coloration. The adult is mostly black above with scattered green spots, changing to green with black-edged scales on the flanks. Its spade-shaped head is black above with irregular yellowish-green streaks. The young are mainly green, with spots of red and white along the back.

Size	To nearly 1 m.
Distribution	Thailand, Malaysia, Indonesia and the Philippines.
Habitat	Forests, where it lives in trees and shrubs.
Food	Lizards, frogs and small mammals.
Breeding	Live-bearing.
Notes	This is the pit viper that is kept on display in the famous snake temple on the island of Penang. **DANGEROUSLY VENOMOUS**

Index

Bracketed numbers refer to species mentioned in the text but not illustrated.

Adder [225], 226
    Death [39], 183
    Desert Death [183]
    Horned 215
    Puff 214
    Spotted Night 220
Aesculapian Snake, 106
Anaconda, Green 51
    Yellow 52

Bandy-bandy 207
Black Snake, Desert 208
Black-headed Snake 167
Blind Snake, Brahminy 23
Boa, African Sand 48
    Amazon Tree 43
    Argentine Rainbow 46
    Baja Californian Rosy 54
    Banana 34
    Brazilian Rainbow 45
    Common 38
    Cuban 44
    Dumeril's 37
    Emerald Tree [58]
    Emerald Tree 42
    Haitian 47
    Javelin Sand 50
    Kenyan Sand [48]
    Madagascan ground [37]
    Mexican Rosy 53
    Pacific 40
    Pacific Ground 39
    Rough-scaled Sand 49
    Round Island 35
    Rubber 41
    Viper 39
Boomslang 98
Bronzeback Snake, Painted 95
Brown Snake, King 204
    Western 205

Bull Snake [114], [76], 154
Burrowing Asp, Corpulent 181
Burrowing snake, Mexican 28
Bush Viper, Hairy 212
Bushmaster 247

Cantil 230
Cat Snake, European [110], 168
Cat-eyed Snake 135
Centipede Snake 161
Centipede-eater, Cape 180
Coachwhip Snake 139
Cobra, Black-necked [196]
    Forest 195
    Indian 197, [198]
    Indonesian Spitting 198
    King 201
    Mozambique Spitting 196
    Spectacled 197
    Spitting 189
Copperhead [114], 231
Copperhead, Australian 185
Coral Snake, African 184
    Arizona 191
    Australian 206
    Blue Malayan 190
    False 116
    South American 194
    Southern 192, [194]
    Texas [80], 193
    Western 191
Corn Snake 104
Cottonmouth [146], 232

Death Adder 183
Desert [183]
DeKay's Snake 165
Dice Snake [140], 142

Egg-eating Snake, African 93
    East African 94

Fer-de-Lance 235
Fierce Snake 202
File snake, Arafurae 25
    Javan [26]
    Small 26

Fishing Snake 115
Fourlined Snake 110
Fox Snake 114

Garter Snake, Black-necked 170
　　　Chequered 172
　　　Eastern 176
　　　Plains 174
　　　Terrestrial 171
Glossy Snake 76
Gopher Snake [76]
　　　Sonoran 152
Grass Snake [140], [142], 141
Green Snake, Rough 147, [148]
　　　Smooth [147], 148
　　　Spotted 150
Ground Python, Calabar 57

Hognose Snake, Eastern [114], 119
　　　Southern 120
　　　Western 118
Hooded Snake [92]
Horseshoe Snake 87
House Snake, Aurora 133
　　　Brown 134

Indigo Snake 99

King Brown Snake 204
Kingsnake, Californian 124
　　　Californian Mountain 132
　　　Desert [124]
　　　Grey Banded 127
　　　Mexican 126
　　　Prairie 123
　　　Sonoran Mountain 128
　　　Speckled 125
Krait, Banded [78]
　　　Banded 186
　　　Sea 209

Ladder Snake 111
Leaf-nosed Snake, Saddled 151
Leopard Snake 113
Long-nosed Snake 159
Lyre Snake 178

Mamba, Black 188

Green 187
Mangrove Snake 78
Massassauga 248
Milksnake, Honduran 130
　　　Pueblan 129
　　　Sinaloan 131
Mole Snake (African) 157
Mole Snake (American) [123]
Montpellier Snake [111], 137
Mulga 204
Mussurana 84

Night Snake, Spotted 121

Palm Viper, Striped 233
Parrot Snake 136
Patch-nosed Snake, Western 160
Pine Snake, Black [153], [99]
　　　Northern 153
　　　Southern [153]
Pipe Snake, Asian 30
　　　South American 29
Pit Viper, Wagler's 252
Python, African 72
　　　Amethystine 64
　　　Angolan [70]
　　　Australian Water [61]
　　　Ball 70
　　　Black-headed 56
　　　Blood 67
　　　Burmese 68
　　　Burmese (albino) 69
　　　Calabar Ground 57
　　　Carpet 66
　　　Centralian Carpet [66]
　　　Children's 60
　　　Diamond 65
　　　Green Tree [42]
　　　Green Tree 58
　　　Macklot's 61
　　　Papuan 63
　　　Pygmy [60]
　　　Reticulated 71
　　　Rough-scaled Carpet [66]
　　　Royal 70
　　　Savu Island [61]
　　　Scrub 64

Spotted 62
Stimson's [62]
White-lipped 59

Racer, American [99], 85
  Red-tailed 117
Rainbow Boa, Argentine 46
  Brazilian 45
Ratsnake, Asiatic 158
  Baird's 100
  Central American 103
  Everglades 109
  Grey 108
  Japanese 102
  Mandarin 107
  Plains 105
  Red 104
  Rosalia 162
  Russian 112
  Texas [108]
  Trans-Pecos 77
  Twin-spotted 101
  Yellow [109]
Rattlesnake, Banded Road 241
  Black-tailed 242
  Canebrake 240
  Eastern Diamondback 236
  Mojave 244
  Pygmy [248] 249
  Red Diamond 243
  South American 239
  Tiger 245
  Western 246
  Western Diamondback 237
Red-bellied Snake 166
Ribbon Snake, Eastern 175
  Western 173
Ringneck Snake 96, [166]
Rinkhals 189
Rosy Boa, Baja Californian 55
  Mexican 53

Sand Boa, African 48
  Javelin 50
  Kenyan [48]
  Rough-scaled 49
Sand Snake, Banded 81

Hissing 156
  Namib 155
Scarlet Snake 80
Sea Snake, Pelagic 210
Shield-nose Snake [184] .
Shovel-nosed Snake
  (American) 82
Shovel-nose Snake
  (Australian) 206
Shovel-nosed Snake,
  Organ Pipe [82]
Sidewinder 238
Slug-eating Snake, Asian 75
  Clouded 163
Smooth Snake 91
  Southern 92
Snail-eating Snake, Catesby's 97
Spitting Cobra 189
  Indonesian 198
  Mozambique 196
Sunbeam snake 27

Taipan [202] 203
Taipan, Inland 202 [203]
Thread snake, Texas, [22]
  Western 22
Tiger Snake, African 169
  Australian 200
  Black 199
  South American 164
Tree Boa, Amazon 43
  Emerald 42, [58]
  Madagascan 55
  Green [42], 58
Tree Snake, Brown 79
Tree Snake, Long-nosed 74
  Paradise 83
Twig Snake 177

Vine Snake 149
Vine Snake, Slender 122
Viper, Aspic 225
  Blunt-nosed [223]
  Carpet 222
  Desert Horned 221
  Eyelash 234
  Gaboon 217

255

Hairy Bush 212
Lataste's 227
Many-horned 216
Milos 223
Nose-horned 224
Palestine 228
Peringuey's 219
Pope's Pit 251
Rhinoceros 218
Russell's 229
Saw-scaled 222
Sedge 213
White-lipped Pit 250
Viperine Snake 140, [142]

Water Snake, Banded 144, [145]
Brown 146
Green 143, [144]
Northern 145
Whipsnake, Balkan 86
Dahl's 89
Dark Green 90
Large 88, [208]
Sonoran 138
Woma [56]
Wood snake, Cuban 33
Haitian 32
Worm snake, European 24